Getting Published

By the same author

The Black Snowman (a collection of poetry)
"How's Business?" "Don't Ask"
Never Make a Reservation in Your Own Name
The Official Guide to Wine Snobbery

Getting Published

THE WRITER IN THE COMBAT ZONE

Leonard S. Bernstein

QUILL · WILLIAM MORROW / NEW YORK

Library of Congress Cataloging-in-Publication Data

Bernstein, Leonard S.
Getting published.

1. Authorship.   2. Authors and publishers.
I. Title.
PN151.B57   1986   808'.02   86-16407
ISBN 0-688-06913-4
ISBN 0-688-06423-X (pbk)

Printed in the United States of America

First Quill Edition

1 2 3 4 5 6 7 8 9 10

BOOK DESIGN BY VICTORIA HARTMAN

for Laura

Contents

PART II   77

Commitment

PART III   101

Preparation

PART IV   117

To the Marketplace

Introduction

THE COMBAT ZONE: This can't refer to writing, can it?
Perhaps we mean the world of business where
confrontation is an everyday event. Perhaps high finance,
where empires topple and fortunes disappear. Perhaps
the tense and aggressive worlds of courtroom law or
politics.

But not writing; writing is the noble profession,
sensitive and distinguished. A world of inspiration, of
elegant thought, of discovery.

And yet writers, in their own curious way, battle for
survival in a creative combat zone as tense and
frustrating as anything found in the business community.
Confined to a frightening solitude and battered by
rejection, they had better have protection—the shrapnel
is flying everywhere.

Indeed, the battleground may be safer for the lawyer
and the businessman. They come to work and at least
something is happening: the phones are ringing; the first
appointment is waiting. The day moves forward on its
track like a locomotive and the lawyer and the
businessman can simply *get on* in the morning. There's
no locomotive for writers, though; they are the
locomotive. And unless they stoke themselves into
motion, there is no motion.

This book is an attempt to understand this strange

phenomenon. The problem demands rethinking; the clichés must be re-examined. Given this understanding, the battlefield becomes a bit safer, a bit less threatening. A path appears among the minefields. Fear lessens, the hide gets thicker, and confidence grows. The emotional straitjacket loosens, and the talent—it was always there —finds a way onto the page. Talent is rarely the problem. A writer's problem is himself, facing the combat zone.

PART I

SELF-DECEPTIONS, MYTHS AND ROADBLOCKS

"We has met the enemy, and it is us."

—Pogo

Never
Show a Story
to a Friend

Writers should have a psychiatrist on retainer. Only a psychiatrist can understand the dreadful insecurities and self-deceptions—those devilish tricks the ego plays—that govern the personality caught in the fever grip of creativity.

Consider: the writer finishes a short story. It's not the first story she's written and she knows it's good. Does she submit it? She does not. She shows it to her best friend. Forget whether her best friend is a fair judge of short stories. Forget whether her friend lives around the block or in the next county; she has the story in her hands before the ink is dry.

"Now, Barbara, I want your absolutely candid opinion," says the writer. "If you hate the story I want you to tell me. If you have any criticisms you have to let me know." In the entire history of the short story, every writer has said exactly those words to her best friend, and the best friend has never answered honestly. How can she? The writer is saying, "Look at my new baby—do you think she's pretty?"

So the friend says she loved the story, which is absolutely meaningless even if she was a judge of stories. And at the

17

same time the friend points out—genuinely trying to be helpful if not candid—that she thinks the beginning can be improved. The writer is surprised but grateful. She had thought the beginning was the best part, but O.K., she was wrong: the beginning has to be changed.

Now here is a writer who knows what she is doing and here is a friend who does not—and the writer changes the beginning of the story. Bring in the psychiatrist; a writing instructor cannot handle this.

The story is changed and it goes out to *McCall's*. No it doesn't; of course not. It goes to the writer's other best friend and the procedure is repeated. The second friend also loves the story but thinks the beginning can be improved. "Oh, let me show you the original version," says the writer, and the friend says the original version is much better.

A third friend loves the story, loves neither beginning, and doesn't think the main character is fully developed. And now the writer is totally disconcerted. A fair rule of writing might be: Never show a short story to a friend unless she's a fiction editor—and I'm not sure about that.

There is probably no absolute standard of excellence for a story unless it is an entirely brilliant piece. Different people, editors included, will react differently to the same manuscript. That should not surprise us. What is the critical reaction to a Broadway show or to a movie? Two people love it, two people hate it, and two more think it's mediocre. Even among professional critics there is a startling disparity of opinion. So why should any two people agree on a short story?

Deep down, writers possibly know this—know that they are the best judges—but are so gripped by uncertainties and so in need of affirmation that they simply cannot accept the story as a completed creative work all by themselves. They travel the seemingly safe but actually dangerous road of showing it around, and end up totally confused and no longer certain of their own feelings. The story has been scissored, pasted, and agonized over, and there is no real sense of improvement. Almost invariably the best thing to do is go back to the original version, close your eyes, and mail it to *McCall's*.

Rejection Slip Scrapbooks

Rejection slips are the most misunderstood part of writing. We all say we hate them when in fact we love them. Why else do we pin them on the walls or paste them in scrapbooks? We love them because in spite of their message they make a clear announcement: *we are writers*.

Of course acceptance letters are better, and personal rejection slips are better than printed rejection slips. We pin the personal rejections front and center. If you ask any writer what he does with rejection slips—into which wastebasket he throws them because after all, why keep them?—you will discover that in spite of all logic he keeps them.

Well, O.K., there's nothing wrong with that. If we can somehow maintain our sanity with a mild ego boost in the intimidating writer's marketplace, why not? At least rejection slips indicate that something is getting written and something is getting submitted.

One of the rewards of writing is that it is a rather distinguished enterprise. We *like* to think of ourselves as writers. Few writers would suffer the indignities of the marketplace if that by-line wasn't so exciting. Rejection slips announce that we *are* writers, and we should listen to the announcement. After all, we're entitled to *something* out of all this pain. In fact we do listen (even if we don't quite understand), and that's why we pin up the slips. Somewhere deep inside we know that rejection slips are in reality acceptances.

Quality Is in the Eye of the Beholder

"Don't ever say that to a young writer," an editor told me. "Quality is what he must strive for."

At first it does sound like a casual approach to writing. Of course quality is what a writer should strive for, as should a doctor, a lawyer and an architect. The problem, in writing, is that the beginner becomes intimidated by the need to *always* produce an exceptional story. It becomes not a striving, but a roadblock. The manuscript does not meet the heavenly standard and the writer retreats, certain that the standard is not reachable. He sends it to *The New*

Yorker and they reject it. Of course they reject it; *The New Yorker* receives 14,000 unsolicited manuscripts a year. But now he is certain that he can never write.

He is so welded to the concept of quality—quality on every page, quality in every paragraph—that he has set an unattainable goal.

It does not occur to the writer that what *The New Yorker* rejects, *Redbook* sometimes accepts. And if both reject it, well perhaps the *Times* will consider it, or one of the city magazines, or one of the airlines magazines—or the local newspaper. Quality is in the eye of the beholder.

If you don't believe that, pick up a current issue of any magazine or any newspaper, and decide for yourself how many articles and stories are "quality." How often have you said to yourself, "I write better than that."? Well, you probably do. The article you just completed, which is not as perfect as you would like it to be, is still as good as the stuff you are reading. Which means, doesn't it, that it is good enough to be published? The problem is that it *can't* be published as long as it is hiding in your bottom drawer waiting to become perfect.

Quality cannot be considered a constant. It does not pour forth relentlessly, unabated. It is not a constant for the beginning writer and it is not a constant for the top-flight professional. The difference is that the professionals know this and accept it. Perhaps a third of what they write is exceptional; the rest is somewhere between good and O.K. After all, the professionals get up at nine every morning and write until one. Every day they turn out 2,000 or 3,000 words, and on some of those days the material sparkles. But no writer ever sparkled constantly. All strive for the exceptional; all achieve it sometimes. But none consider constant exceptional performance the condition of success. If they did, they would be unable to function. Even after editing and rewriting, the piece may be less than the professional would prefer. If the piece is really inadequate, it might be destroyed, or more likely put in deep freeze, in the hope of thawing it out at a more inspired moment. If the piece is adequate but not outstanding, it might be sent to a lesser journal. Not every story has to be published in *Redbook* or *The New Yorker*.

A writer (may the literary societies forgive me) is like a baseball player. The ballplayer goes to bat, and the chances are only three in ten that he will get a hit. The writer, in equal measure, sits at the typewriter, and the chances are only three in ten that *he* will get a hit. The ballplayer, however, does not collapse emotionally after the seven times he does not get a hit. In fact, three in ten is a batting average of .300, which is damn good and way ahead of most of the players who are only batting .250.

If only the writer could see it that way, but he can't. The seven times that he doesn't get a hit seem to him like failure.

He has no concept of the .300 batting average. Naturally he doesn't because writers do not have their batting averages printed in the paper every day as ballplayers do. Ballplayers can *see* that .300 means they are in the top 5 percent. Writers can't see anything. If there were a way for writers to understand what is respectable in terms of quality and acceptance, there would be a lot more healthy egos in the literary fraternity. So the concept of quality, on its surface a most admirable objective, paralyzes the beginning writer because he cannot regularly attain it. You can hear him saying that, perhaps in slightly different words, "I've been working on this short story for four months. I'm into the fifth draft. I think I might be getting it now."

On the surface, not unreasonable. But invariably he will be working on the same story four months later. He can't complete it and submit it because he can't get it perfect. If another month *will* get it perfect, take the month. Take six weeks; anything to get it perfect. But in fact it never will be because after six months it is probably as perfect as he can make it. And after all, if we are writers, we must do more than two pieces a year.

Consider: how many of anything is consistently flawless? Businessmen and lawyers have their inspired, enthusiastic and brilliant days. Otherwise their performance is average. Architects design brilliant homes, but most of the homes they design never make it into *House Beautiful*. Ballplayers sometimes get four hits in a game, but most of the time they get one.

So it follows that inconsistency must be tolerated. We are grateful for the story that turns out exceptional, but we accept the story that does not. We wrap them both up and send them out into the cruel marketplace, obviously aiming a little higher with the exceptional. Editors have entirely different ideas about which stories are exceptional. *Quality is in the eye of the beholder.*

Understanding
the Marketplace

At the roulette wheel in Atlantic City a seasoned gambler is playing number 39. The wheel spins, the ball lodges in number 5, and the gambler loses. Of course he loses; there are fifty numbers on the wheel. The odds against him are fifty to one.

He decides to play again, this time betting on *black*. The wheel spins and the ball falls into a red slot. The gambler has lost again, and this time he is visibly annoyed. Of course he's annoyed; half the slots are red and half are black. He had a fifty-fifty chance.

The encyclopedia salesman canvases a neighborhood. He knocks on twenty doors and is hardly listened to. Does he surrender, convinced that his efforts cannot possibly pay? Of course he doesn't; somewhere ahead of him is a door that will open and an encyclopedia set that will be sold. He has only to trust in persistence and a reasonable estimate of probabilities.

The baseball player does not expect to hit a home run every time at bat; the insurance salesman does not expect to sell a policy with each phone call. But the writer, buoyed by the most remarkable expectations, sends a short story to *Redbook* and expects it to be accepted.

In fact, these are the probabilities: During the year 1985 *Redbook* received 25,000 unsolicited short story manuscripts. Five were chosen for publication. The odds were therefore 5,000 to 1. Let us assume that of the 25,000 stories, 24,000 were mediocre and only 1,000 were really possibilities, and let us assume that our manuscript was among the 1,000. Now the odds have been reduced to 200 to 1. Why then does the writer send a story to *Redbook* and expect it to be accepted? More important, why, when it is not accepted, are we so disappointed and disillusioned that we stop writing for a year?

Exaggeration? Just a bit perhaps. But in any writing course it can be observed that perfectly competent writers take one shot at a major magazine and then give up.

Well, why shouldn't they give up? Why should they have even tried in the first place? What is the answer to such a discouraging marketplace?

There are many answers: the first is to try markets where the odds are not so overwhelming. There are smaller, less competitive magazines than *Redbook* and there are hundreds of literary journals. The October issue of *The Writer* lists 110 markets for short stories without even including the literary journals.

The second answer is that although the odds may be staggering for a single short story, they are cut exactly in half with two short stories and improve dramatically with ten short stories. A serious writer does not market a single story (as an encyclopedia salesman does not knock on a single door). A writer writes stories and submits them to the larger marketplace. If we persist, we get published. In ten years of teaching writing courses I have never known a competent writer who continued to write and continued to submit and did not get published. And let's be clear about this: I don't mean a marvelously talented writer; I mean a competent writer. Most of the writers in any writing course are competent. On the other hand I know marvelously talented writers who sent their single short story to *Redbook* and have never been published.

The rule is this: *Understand the probabilities and don't get discouraged.* Getting published is not as easy as it seems when you send out your first story, and not as difficult as it seems after you have had five stories rejected. It is involved with probabilities—with odds—like the gambler, the salesman, the ballplayer and most other endeavors in our lives.

The Rule of Twelve

The laws of probability—the "odds"—can be arranged to work *for* writers as well as against them. If the gambler bets every number on the fifty-number roulette wheel, he has a winner with each spin. Similarly, if the writer keeps enough manuscripts in the marketplace, the formidable odds against a single submission improve dramatically. If the odds are twelve to one against a single manuscript, then with twelve manuscripts in the marketplace theoretically one must be accepted.

Obviously it doesn't work quite as neatly as that, as any writer who has suffered twenty rejections on a single story will tell you. But then for every story that gets rejected twenty times there is the story that only gets rejected four times. Thus two stories collect twenty-four rejections—an *average* of twelve rejections a story.

So certainly the writer whose story has been rejected five times should hardly be bringing his typewriter to the pawnshop. He has not even begun to experience the realities of the marketplace.

To which a writer might respond, "Who wants to experience the realities of the marketplace if those are the realities?"

Well, O.K., no one said you have to play the game. If you can't accept the rules you are always welcome to drop out. But at least drop out after you *do* understand the rules. Don't submit a story three times, to the top magazines in America, and then surrender after three rejections. First of all that's naive; second it's cowardly; and third you are not being true to your own talent. Three rejections mean absolutely nothing. If you're going to drop out after three you might as well not start.

Which brings us, via a somewhat roundabout path, to THE RULE OF TWELVE. This is a rule of probabilities and it is designed to suggest a rational approach to the marketplace. You don't dive out the window if the lottery doesn't pay off, and you don't start looking over the ledge when the story comes back—yes, with a printed rejection slip—from *The Atlantic*.

In fact, almost the opposite is true. Almost all manuscripts, competently written, are publishable. It remains for the writer to find the right strata of publications, and then to pound on enough doors.

THE RULE OF TWELVE contends that every competent (not extraordinary) story or article will be accepted after a certain number of times submitted. Let's say twelve times, although twelve is obviously arbitrary. It depends on the writer's talent and the strata of the magazines he submits to. Some writers will have an average times-out of seventeen. Others will have six. If the seventeen-times-out writer lowers the sights a little, the number reduces to twelve. If the six-times-out writer only aims for *Playboy* and *The Atlantic*, the number goes up to twelve.

This doesn't mean that every story or article gets accepted on the twelfth submission. It means that the average is twelve; the RULE is twelve. Some stories will get accepted on the seventh submission; some on the seventeenth.

The point is the RULE does work. The pity is that few writers follow it.

THE RULE OF TWELVE therefore means that if the writer has twelve manuscripts out in the marketplace, one of them will be accepted. It also means that if there is only one manuscript out, *it* will be accepted—but not until the twelfth time out. And if there are only six manuscripts circulating, one of those will be accepted the second time around. Twelve manuscripts presented; one manuscript accepted. That's the RULE.

A writer who has less than six pieces out should be paying less attention to the probabilities of acceptance, and more attention to writing.

There are exceptions: THE RULE OF TWELVE utilizes rational probabilities *if* the writer is tuned to the marketplace. If the same story travels to *Playboy* and *Ladies' Home Journal*, scratch one of those two chances. One of them is a no-chance.

Being tuned to the marketplace also means being aware that the articles market does not end with the top ten magazines in the front of the newsstand. If you spin *that* roulette wheel the odds go from twelve to one to perhaps twenty-four to one. There's nothing wrong with trying; there is nothing lost by shooting high except stamps and time, but you should understand the possibilities. Behind the top ten come countless excellent journals, including newspapers, national and local, city magazines, airlines magazines, religious magazines, sports magazines, and specialized magazines of every description. It is really impossible to run out of markets; it can only be done if the manuscript becomes dated, and that is not a fault of the marketplace.

I genuinely believe that THE RULE OF TWELVE is not applicable if you are only submitting a piece or two. It is somewhat like betting a single roulette number over and over. You could sit at the wheel all night and never be a winner. As a matter of pure probability, you must hit that number one time out of however many numbers are on the wheel. But probabilities require a larger mix to work.

Indeed, it takes stamina. It takes persistence and determination. But it helps to know that somewhere down that road there are probabilities that work. I think it is the one thing that can sustain the writer in the terribly cruel world of the marketplace.

At the risk of overstating my case, I'm going to illustrate on page 30 the RULE as it actually might appear in a writer's records.

Story #1, which the writer did not bury, was rejected eleven times and then accepted on the 12th submission. Par for the course.

Story #2 was not accepted within this schedule, but that does not mean it was not accepted. Barring an untimely subject, this story gets accepted on the 27th or 34th submission.

x = rejection
A = acceptance

Magazine #	1	2	3	4	5	6	7	8	9	10	11	12	13	14	15	16	17	18	19	20
Story #1	x	x	x	x	x	x	x	x	x	x	x	A								
Story #2	x	x	x	x	x	x	x	x	x	x	x	x	x	x	x	x	x	x	x	x
Story #3	x	x	x	x	x	x	x	x	x	x	x	x	x	x	x	x	x	A		
Story #4	x	x	x	x	x	x	A													
Story #5	x	x	x	x	x	x	x	x	x	x	x	x	x	x	x	x	x	x	x	A
Article #6	x	A																		
Article #7	x	x	x	x	x	x	x	x	x	x	x	x	x	A						
Article #8	x	x	x	x	x	x	x	x	A											
Article #9	x	x	x	A																
Article #10	x	x	x	x	x	x	x	x	x	x	x	x	x	x	x	x	x	x	x	x

THE RULE OF TWELVE states that if you submit a competent manuscript to appropriate and realistic markets, it will, *on average*, be accepted on the 12th time out.

The above chart represents the acceptance/rejection record of a competent freelance writer, possibly yourself. If you look at the x's, you will give up writing and take up stamp collecting. If you look at the A's, you will note that eight of ten manuscripts have been *accepted*.

Story #3 is accepted on the 18th time out. Story #4, on the 7th.

Story #5 sneaks in on the 20th time out—just before you were about to give up. Never give up.

Article #6 is accepted on the 2nd trip. Try more articles.

Article #7—a standard RULE OF TWELVE acceptance on the 14th spin.

Article #8—another standard result—the 9th.

Article #9 is accepted on the 4th time out, which is a big surprise because you thought article #9 was pretty mediocre and destined for the outer extreme of the chart.

Article #10 is not accepted at all. Not on the 20th submission. Not on the 40th. Who told you to write about Watergate?

♦ ♦ ♦

There it is, a realistic picture of the probabilities. Lots of submissions; not many acceptances. You can look at the x's and get discouraged, but you can also look at the A's. There are eight acceptances on this chart; eight magazines or newspapers that carry your by-line. All this time you thought you would never be published, and here you are —almost a professional.

The Calvin Coolidge Approach

"Nothing in the world can take the place of persistence. Talent will not; nothing is more common than unsuccessful men with talent. Genius will not; unrewarded genius is almost a proverb. Education will not; the world is full of educated derelicts. Persistence and determination alone are omnipotent."

—Calvin Coolidge

Why should it be that we have to use words like "persistence" and "determination" to talk about writing? Why can't we use poetic and creative words to describe the creative process?

Because although the products of the craft are poetic and creative, the *process* of creation is an incredibly difficult and disciplined undertaking.

There is nothing more difficult than writing a story, simply because the writer begins with nothing. He has a blank sheet of paper, a typewriter, and an idea. Nothing is started; there is no format, no procedure. He must bring it all forth from a vacuum.

Consider that the doctor arrives in his office at nine o'clock, and his day begins for him. There is a patient and an ailment, and he responds to this circumstance mechanically and intellectually, and then goes on to the next patient. In between there are phone calls, and finally there is a trip to the hospital: in all cases a response to an event.

The businessman arrives in his office and immediately gets on the same merry-go-round. The Sears Roebuck buyer calls to place an order. The factory calls to report a production-line breakdown. The accountant calls to discuss the balance sheet. Yes, certainly the businessman may find a quiet hour to design and create a new product, but that is a *breakaway* from the schedule that drives him through the day.

Even the artist can set his easel in front of a forest and paint what he sees or some distortion of what he sees. Which is why artists have classically set up still lifes or worked from models, so they would have something to respond to, something to help them generate.

But the writer generates from nothing.

He enters that cold, demanding room—four walls, a typewriter, and paper—and he must do it all. No one calls with a problem to respond to. There is no program, no schedule; there are no people. There is nothing but the bouncing of electric currents in the brain, and very often there are not too many of them. The solitude is frightening.

And that is why the doctor and the businessman can put in a day's work. The events carry them along, whether they are creative or not. The writers, so very often, do nothing. Of course they do nothing, because it is so damn difficult to do something.

The professional writers understand this and get into the

habit of confronting the blank piece of paper. From nine in the morning to one or two in the afternoon, they put something down. They have no merry-go-round to climb upon, like the doctor and the businessman, but over the years they have become disciplined.

These being the rules of the game, it is not surprising that persistence, discipline and determination play a large part—a larger part than talent—in the generation of the written idea.

There is a poet who claims that when she is without an idea, she opens the encyclopedia and reads quickly about the first animal or insect she comes to. Then she doesn't get out of her chair until she writes a poem about that creature. She insists that animals have led her into all kinds of intriguing thoughts—about survival, about culture patterns—and have triggered some of her best poetry. She also contends (and this is particularly important) that the device serves as an assignment: She *knows* what she is going to write about before she sits down.

There is another writer who in that state of frenzied noninspiration writes grocery lists. He says that writing grocery lists is better than not writing anything, and furthermore, once he gets started on a grocery list—once he starts moving the pencil across the pad—he finds that it leads to something.

Both writers argue that in the absence of these admittedly crass devices or disciplines they are likely to spend their time at their writing desk trying to decide whether to write about *death* or *happiness*, two subjects likely to send them back and forth from the cookie jar.

The
Big Mac
Approach

The How-to article is to writing as McDonald's is to restaurants; it enjoys no status. Nevertheless, McDonald's advertises 50 BILLION SOLD, a point the writer might keep in mind.

The writer reacts to the How-to article with discomfort and disdain as though it were a violation of the craft, a sacrilege. Here the writer sits, thinking about writing *The Naked and the Dead*. Can he possibly consider "How to Make a Chocolate Mousse"?

And who would not agree that he *should* write *The Naked and the Dead* if he can. But meanwhile he should write *something*, because that's what a writer does. And in that context there is much to be said for the lowly How-to article.

Let's admit right away that it is not the most demanding exercise of the writer's skill. Let's concede that it does not aspire to literary immortality. But let's not be smug; there are more How-to articles published every month in respectable magazines than any other kind. And that simply means that there are more How-to articles being read.

Somewhere I hear voices saying that there are also a lot of pulp stories and true romances published every month, and doesn't that mean that the writer should write formula true romance stories? I think not. I think there is a discernible difference in quality. A How-to article can be articulate and fascinating, which is just what the How-tos in *Family Circle, House Beautiful,* and *Ladies' Home Journal* are.

There is another argument—persuasive, I think: a How-to article can always be *written.* So after the writer has considered *The Snows of Kilimanjaro* for six months and has written nothing, it's time to think mundane thoughts like what is possible.

I always know when I should write a How-to article (which is not to say that I always write one). After I've marched back and forth from the refrigerator six times in an hour —after I've sharpened all the pencils around my desk— then it's time. The Great American Novel has eluded me again. A pity, but it's not the first time. Maybe tomorrow. Meanwhile, if only to avoid a humiliating encounter with my bathroom scale, it's time to write a How-to.

And of course I can always write one, and so can everybody else. It is the easiest article to write (though not necessarily to write effectively) because it requires only that the writer know how to do something well enough to relate it in an engaging manner. If you ask around a writing class you will hear fifteen writers say that there is *nothing* they know well enough, but O.K., it's possible to get past that. Allowed thirty minutes with any writer, you find that there are ten things she knows well enough to write about. Of course she does; what does she *talk* about during the day?

There are very few people who cannot write five articles about money: how to save it intelligently; how to spend it frivolously; how to lose it in the stock market; how to make it back in Atlantic City. How to pay your taxes; how to avoid paying taxes; how to balance your checkbook; how to get your spouse to balance the checkbook.

A good way to approach how-tos, and also to cut calories, is to make a list of possibilities and tack it up on your desk. Then you'll *know* what you're going to write next. If that doesn't work, purchase the current issue of *Good Housekeeping* and choose one of the subjects in that issue. Dieting is a good example. There has never been an issue of *Good Housekeeping* that didn't have a dieting article. That's because there are fifty million dieters in America, and the odds are about even that you are (or were) one of them. So write: "How to Lose Twelve Pounds on an Artichoke Diet." Or write: "How to Gain Twelve Pounds on an Artichoke Diet." If the result is any good, you have an audience of fifty million and you'll never run out of magazines and newspapers to send it to.

There are certain guidelines to the How-to article. Violate all of them if you'd like to; rules are a guide, not a prison. But if you care to consider what usually works, here are some ideas:

1. A How-to article must convey skill. It must convince the reader that you know how to do it. Even a How-not-to—a parody or a burlesque—demands that the writer know his way around the area.

2. A How-to article must have a position, a slant, a unique angle. It can't resemble the instructions for model planes; nobody will read it.

3. A How-to article bounces right along. It has pace; it doesn't dwell. The subject matter is generally neither

urgent nor philosophical and it demands a style consistent with the content.

Obviously there are exceptions. If you are telling how to raise a handicapped child, this is no place for levity. But that is rarely the problem. The common error is to load down a fast-moving article with ponderous considerations and historical precedents.

4. The How-to article, previously defined as nonphilosophical, does not require circuitous routes to the main point. In-depth analysis, particularly at the beginning, is certain to lose the reader. Instead, charge right into the subject. Get the play onto centerstage. Swing away. Avoid prefaces, wind-ups, weather reports, and descriptions of the countryside. Sacrifice mood and nostalgia for action.

Remember that you are taking a position. You have an angle. State it right away while the reader is giving you a chance.

5. Narrow your subject matter. It is not possible to write an article on "How to Be an Expert Cook." The scope is too wide. That's material for a book. Instead, write "How to Cook Spaghetti," or "How to Ruin Spaghetti," or "How to Eat Spaghetti." If you're a karate expert, don't write about the art of self-defense. Consider "Karate for the Ten-Year-Old."

6. A How-to article must challenge your readers. It must make them want to do it; it must generate enthusiasm. If readers can't live the part, they'll turn to an article they can live.

At the very least readers must be provoked. If you

can't win them, you might as well lose them; you might as well drive them to thinking that *nobody* would want to do that.

7. Finally, a How-to article is not a manual. It should sparkle with the personality of the writer. It should bristle, cajole, irritate, endear. It should be spirited, because it is spirit that lights the reader's imagination.

That's what a How-to article *ought* to be, and it leaves more room for literary adventure and experiment than most writers imagine. It is not crass, it is not mundane, and it is not a sell-out. Above all, people like to read them, and consequently the best magazines are constantly looking for creative How-tos. It follows, then, if writers would like to find themselves in the best magazines, that they should at least give the How-to a try.

The Flaw Mentality

She was in her mid-thirties, talented, and taking a course in "Writing for Publication." It was not a beginner's course; it assumed that the writer had been producing manuscripts over the months or over the years, and that she was now ready to cross the bridge from casual, once-in-a-while writing to a serious attempt at getting published.

It was her turn, that night, to read her manuscript to the group, and to have it criticized. It was a stylish, intriguing story, and although there were one or two minor suggestions the group was enthusiastic.

"Have you sent that story out?" the instructor asked.

"No, I haven't. I'm still working on it. This is about my fifth draft; I can't seem to get it just right."

"I thought the group found it just right, and I did also," he answered.

"No they didn't. Roger thought the main character needed development, and Virginia said that the part about the automobile trip was irrelevant. The story still has flaws. I'm going home to correct them."

"I'm not arguing against correcting flaws," said the instructor, "but you mentioned that you were into the fifth draft. How long have you been working on the story?"

The writer lowered her eyes and it was obvious that the instructor might have found a more gentle route to that question. But it was asked, and she answered it. "I've been working on the story for two years."

At this point the instructor hesitated. It was apparent that acute sensibilities were on the line. Wisely he threw it out to the class: "Will anyone comment on why Deborah continues to edit, and hesitates to submit a story we all feel is so compelling?"

An explanation came from Nina, another student, and it was then that the instructor learned about "the flaw mentality."

"Deborah is finding flaws in her manuscript so she will not *have to* send it out," Nina said. "A lot of us do that. We don't want to face the marketplace. We're afraid of the rejections, the neglect, the anguish, the put-downs. So we keep our stories and articles in a state of constant incompletion. If they are completed, we all know very well that we should send them out."

The instructor marveled at her perception.

"That's why," she continued, "we always find flaws. As long as a story has a flaw, the flaw has to be corrected and the story is incomplete. We can find a flaw in any story. I remember when Deborah first wrote that story; we were taking a Creative Writing course together. She read the story to the group, and the group thought it was terrific, just like tonight. Of course there were suggestions; someone said the beginning wasn't strong enough or perhaps the main character was too developed. I don't remember exactly. Deborah did a little editing—I don't think she'll mind me telling this because we all do the same thing—and read it again in another Creative Writing class a year later. Same enthusiasm, same suggestions."

The instructor looked around the room and was amazed. Fifteen writers were smiling and nodding, and generally voicing approval, as though someone were reading from the Bible. It was apparent that Nina had touched upon a universal problem and a universal hang-up.

The instructor pushed forward. "At the last session we read two stories, Arthur's and Jennifer's. When were *those* stories completed?"

Arthur didn't mind answering; a central nerve had been touched. "I finished my story about nine months ago."

"And why didn't you send it out?"

"Because it still needs work. It still has flaws."

"But nine months to correct the flaws, Arthur, surely . . ."

"Well, I correct some and then I find others. And then I'm not sure about some of the corrections so I change them around. I can't seem to get it just right."

"I think I told you that the story was excellent, and I think I suggested that you submit it to one of the quarterlies."

"You did," said Arthur, "but you also bracketed a paragraph that you said I could live without."

"Well, presuming that you agree with me—and you don't have to, you know—that would only require retyping."

Jennifer's story had traveled the same road: written a year ago, rewritten twice, and then sat upon. Resurrected under the protective umbrella of repeated writing classes. Inevitably flaw-marked; forever improvable. But Jennifer ventured a courageous admission:

"Maybe the flaw is not within our stories, but within ourselves. Certainly I could have finished this story a year ago. Certainly I could have been submitting it. Even those flaws that it does have I could have edited in an hour. It's obvious to me, after what we have been saying, that something is holding me back from completing the story. Whatever it is, causes me to perceive the flaws as a device for keeping the story incomplete."

"Yet you're not unwilling to read the story to the group?"

"Different matter," said Jennifer. "The group is warm and comfortable. We all know about rejection slips. We all know how the writer suffers. There's a camaraderie."

"A womb. An incubation," challenged Margaret from across the room.

"Yes, even that, I suppose," admitted Jennifer. "Whatever it is, it's supportive. It's close to home; it's within the family. It's not the cruel world outside."

The writing session had taken a curious turn, and now sounded more like a psychology course.

It happens that there was a psychologist among the writers, and she was amazed at the revelations. "If I didn't have so many hang-ups about my own writing," she said, "I would have figured this out long ago. I'm still correcting a story from three years ago.

"I have some thoughts about this flaw mentality," she continued. "I think I know why we do it, and since everyone here is being candid, I'd like to toss out some ideas.

"These stories and poems are very close to our hearts, closer than we understand. They are all that we stand for as individuals. We perceive ourselves as writers, and it's a glorious perception. If you asked us the single thing we would most like to be, and if we were honest, we would answer: published writers. If we are with people we have just met, the anxiety tugs at us: to announce ourselves as writers. It's the ego peg that we hang our hats on, our very badge of honor. We are immensely proud of our talent and incredibly vulnerable in its fragility. We are an emotional house of cards; you can collapse us with a breath.

"I hardly think this should come as a surprise. Notice how inflated we become when an instructor praises our manuscripts. And notice how crushed we are when they are found to be mediocre. It's all out of proportion. Mediocre means that *we* are mediocre. When a person hangs his identity on a single ego peg, the whole identity rises and falls on a single circumstance. A manuscript, then, is beyond a manuscript.

"It follows that rejection is not simply rejection of a story, but rejection on a grander scale. And it further follows that the writer does not want to be subject to it. Better not to ask the beauty queen out, than to ask her out and have her say no.

"So the writer develops this flaw mentality to avoid courting the beauty queen, to avoid the editors of *Esquire* and *Harper's.*

"It amazes me," the psychologist continued, "that I can be perceptive and articulate about this problem, and yet I'm hooked beyond salvation."

♦ ♦ ♦

Usually a writing instructor leads a class. Sometimes a class leads an instructor. This was surely one of those times. The instructor made notes and listened carefully as a whole new approach to writing poured forth from an expert source.

In future classes with different writers, he discussed the flaw mentality, hoping that the writers might sense this curious, almost bizarre, problem. He did his best to indicate that stories and articles, although obviously important to the writer, were *not* the whole identity, but were stories and articles. He urged the writers to submit their manuscripts just so that they would *get used to* rejection slips. He theorized that once you go through the pain of asking out the beauty queen, it's much easier the second time.

In future classes he insisted that manuscripts would *have to be* submitted, firmly believing that he had nothing as valuable to give his students as the tools to fight the flaw mentality. The students resisted; the instructor hammered away; and finally the writers closed their eyes and dived into the deep end of the pool.

Eventually they discovered that the water was not as cold as they thought. Some jumped right out again; some stayed in a while; some found that they could swim around the pool, and they were delighted.

The instructor was also delighted, believing that he had discovered, and was communicating, something important.

And with each writing group he confirmed, with even greater certainty, the existence of the flaw mentality, and set out to see what he could do about it.

The Writer in Trouble

Coupled with the flaw mentality is another device that writers use to circumvent the pain of writing and submitting: the creative writing course. Writers string together a lifetime of writing courses and delude themselves into thinking they are writing. A quick count of their production tells the story: Writers who continually frequent writing courses have only a few stories and articles completed. They think of themselves as writers because a writing course sounds as if writing is going on. The proof, however, is in the manuscripts.

The problem is not in the individual writing course. Every writer can profit from one course given by an inspired teacher. The problem is with *continued* writing courses. Just as, in the flaw mentality, a manuscript can be more than a manuscript, a writing course can be more than a writing course. It can be a haven, a hideout; and it usually is.

In fairness, there are two ways of looking at the writing course: It can be social or it can be serious. Social means you take the course to meet interesting people; you spend an evening out; you listen to stories and articles, and maybe you do a little writing. At least you know why you're there.

The second possibility involves the students who are serious. They consider themselves writers or potential writers, and are taking the course to write. If it's their first course, it's a good idea. If it's their second or third, they may be in trouble.

There are a number of signs announcing writers-in-trouble. The first is simply that they are taking their third writing course when they should be home writing. That is a bit unfair; if they have manuscripts to show for the three writing courses, the courses are obviously helping. It is invariably my experience, however, that writers, in their third writing course, do not have the manuscripts. Certainly they have a half dozen stories or articles, but the courses have spread over two years. One story every four months is not serious writing.

The second sign indicating writers-in-trouble is that they bring old stories into the new writing class. After all, you have to bring *something* into a writing class—ideally something that you are writing. If you bring, instead, something you have written, it doesn't add up to production. When writers, during the first few weeks, bring the instructor manuscripts long completed, there is cause for concern. What they are doing is "showcasing": letting the instructor see their trophies instead of showing him how well they can play the game. Letting him see what they have done, instead of doing it. This is an ailment among writers as common as tennis elbow among tennis players. In tennis, it usually means that you are not hitting the ball properly, and in writing it means the same thing.

The third sign of trouble rears its head during the last week or two of a ten-week writing course. Students will ask the instructor: "When are you giving the course again?"

It is not instruction that the students seek, but protection. Just as the flaw mentality weaves a warm nest for the writers, so does the writing course. As long as they are there, they can be learning. Once they leave the nest, they must spread their wings and fly.

I suppose both student and instructor might learn from the mother eagle. She knows that the fledgling will stay forever in the nest. So one day she lifts him out and forces him into the open sky, knowing instinctively that his wings are developed, and that he can use them.

The final indication of writers-in-trouble is the passing around of manuscripts. It is only the second week of the writing course and some writers have asked half the class to criticize their work. Immediately I know that I will get very little from them. Again, they are interested, not in writing, but in presenting themselves as writers. They take a writing course, presumably with serious intent, but in fact, to massage their egos.

If I had the courage, I would announce during the first week of a writing course that no manuscript already completed could be brought into the class, either to myself or to another student. I expect that such an edict would send fifteen writers down to the registrar's office for refunds. Along with the requests for refund would be accusations of insensitivity and tyranny. Still, I think it would be the single best thing for each of the fifteen writers.

As another approach, I might insist that any stories or articles previously completed could be brought in for criticism only during the tenth week. In such event, the writer would have no choice but to write during the first nine.

I hold to the idea that a writing course is neither an ego

trip nor a trophy showcase, but a working operation. And I hold further that this working operation is to the writer as law school is to the future lawyer, a rite of passage that will enable the student to practice law.

Falling in Love

We are in the second week of a ten-week writing seminar. Richard hands in a writing assignment that's excellent, but three or four pages too long.

"Cut the twenty pages to sixteen or seventeen," suggests the instructor, pointing out expendable passages, "and you'll have a publishable article."

Two weeks later the instructor asks whether Richard has edited the manuscript, and whether it's on some editor's desk. He hasn't; he says he's working on it.

We know this could be *the flaw mentality* at work: the finding and maintaining of a flaw in a manuscript so it will *not have to be* submitted. But it could be something else. It could be another bit of perverse psychology: The writer might have *fallen in love* with his manuscript.

Yes, that's what we do: We fall in love with our manuscripts. Never mind that we bury them in the bottom drawer. Never mind the protests of inadequacy when we hand one to the writing instructor. Somewhere, deep down and inexplicable, the love affair blossoms. So that finally, when the writer is asked what is delaying the editing and sub-mitting of the manuscript, the answer is: "What can I pos-sibly cut?"

No writing instructor can cure this malady because it is unrelated to writing. This requires advice to the lovelorn. This is like telling your seventeen-year-old daughter to break up with her boyfriend because he's obviously no good for her. Good sense and logic do not work; you must find your way into her heart.

I don't suggest that I know the cure, but I have suffered the malady. On various occasions I have received back from editors a 3,000-word manuscript with the notation: "We like it. Cut it to 2,000 words and we'll buy it."

My immediate reaction is outrage. "Cut it to 2,000 words? It was meant to be 3,000 words! How about artistic integrity? This is my *manuscript*, damn it. I sweated over this."

After my anger subsides, I move into my I WON'T DO IT mood. If they don't like the piece the way I wrote it, I'll send it to another magazine that does. This mood generally lasts two or three days. The explanation? I've fallen in love with my manuscript.

After two or three days of "I won't do it!" I adjust into "I'll think about it." A few realities have presented them-selves:

1. The manuscript has already been *rejected* four times. Nobody is standing on line to buy it.

2. The subject matter is *current*. Six months from now it will be stale.

3. There might be, I concede, an outside possibility that I *could* cut two or three hundred words.

Another day passes, and what is actually happening is that my ardor is cooling. I still don't agree with the editor but I am now courting two lovers: I'm in love with my article and I'm in love with the idea of seeing it in print. Literary bigamy. I soon start to think that if I can cut three hundred words, I can cut six hundred words, and cursing (although not loudly), I get started.

It's genuinely difficult to cut; everything is good. However, that's not the test. The test is: Something has to go —what shall it be? This is an emotional problem, not a writing problem. Once I've *accepted* the advice-to-the-lovelorn, the rest is easy. I finish the editing and put away the article—to put some space between us—intending to read it tomorrow.

"Tomorrow" a strange thing happens: I read the article and I don't really notice anything missing. In fact, I'm forced to admit that it seems to move along with a little more energy and pace. The editor, it appears, was right. And not only right about what is wanted for space allotment, but right about the article. Well, naturally I'm not prepared to admit that editors know more than writers, but at least editors do not fall in love with manuscripts—except probably their own.

So I've gone through the shattered love affair and I've emerged undamaged, not to speak of $500 richer and with a by-line which I will immediately Xerox and send to everybody I've known since the fourth grade.

I tell the story to Richard and hope that he will *now* cut three pages from his manuscript. He probably will not. My story will not break up his love affair. After all, my editor's advice didn't break up mine. It was the *alternative* that broke up mine. Another woman entered the picture.

I wish I had the other woman for Richard; that would bust things up. And maybe she will appear. Maybe Richard will submit his story at twenty pages and some editor will tell him to cut a thousand words. Richard will see his name in bright lights—that's a mighty seductive other woman— and he'll cut four pages out of that story within fifteen minutes.

"What's going on here?" you have a right to ask. "I thought this was about writing. If I want advice to the lovelorn I'll read *Dear Abby*." Indeed, you're correct, but writing doesn't have much to do with writing. It has to do with emotions, roadblocks, smokescreens, love affairs. It has to do with manuscripts, yes, but they are fragments of the heart, dearer to us than we can possibly understand.

Semi-colons and Ellipses

The evil god of Grammar haunts the lives of writers and would-be writers, strangling them with a discipline that they cannot bear, do not recognize, and feel is useless. So it is hardly a surprise, when the manuscripts are handed in at a writing seminar, that nobody knows whether the comma comes before or after the quotation mark; nobody knows the difference between a dash and a hyphen; and absolutely nobody knows what an ellipsis is. Even if they do know that an ellipsis is those funny-looking dots that suggest a pause in the prose line, some writers use two dots, some writers six dots, and some writers vary their dots depending upon how long a pause they wish to suggest. It is not unlike those writers who use two and three question marks, depending upon the complexity of the question.

The notion that grammar is a tool of writing escapes too many writers; they feel it is a prison, intended to wall them in and constrict their natural creativity. And while good grammar doesn't make good writers, the *approach* to grammar is important. Writers who feel that good grammar is beneath them—is a waste of creative time—are self-indulgent and lazy. They want to skip the ground rules, skip the training programs, skip the apprenticeship, and arrive fully matured in the pages of *The New Yorker*.

Coupled with their approach to grammar is their attitude toward spelling: "The editors will fix it up if they like it."

It's true, grammar is tedious. But lots of things are tedious: piano practice, language courses, training programs of every type. We endure them so that we can learn a skill which, finally developed, is not tedious at all.

The Writer Incapacitated

I am embarrassed to admit how often I've pleaded Writer's Block when I know damn well there is no such thing. But how else is a writer to explain those stretches of inactivity, those communions with the refrigerator? Laziness? Self-indulgence? Of course not. Instead, being an imaginative group, we invent a noble excuse: a rare, exotic and fashionable infirmity called Writer's Block.

Notice what a lovely name we have chosen. Immediately it announces that we are Writers (when in fact we aren't writing anything). Immediately it announces that we are special: members of an exclusive group. And then consider Block: an insurmountable barrier. No way to get around it. We are forgiven.

Writers are terribly adept at a number of things. Writing may not be one of them, but rationalizing surely is. Writers can rationalize themselves around anything. Which is why we don't want to hear the solution to Writer's Block; it is too distressing, too banal, too inelegant. The solution is: Write something. At once the defense lines up: "If we could write something, then we wouldn't be suffering from Writer's Block for godsakes."

Nevertheless, illnesses are treated with medicine and medicine rarely tastes good. The solution to Writer's Block is similarly distasteful and does not improve because we wish it so. One approach is to write a grocery list—a list of fifty items that you might purchase at the supermarket: apples, oranges, bananas. While you are at it try for a little melody. Apples-oranges-bananas sounds better than oranges-bananas-apples. If you want to know why you must endure this humiliation, it is to keep the writing mechanism oiled up—unblocked, you might say.

If groceries seem beneath the creative spirit, try artists:

> Giotto, Botticelli, Pollock,
> Ben Benn, Shinn, Ben Shahn, Picasso

If you can't get yourself to do groceries *or* artists, be wary. It suggests that you might enjoy Writer's Block as some people enjoy their illnesses, removing them from the responsibilities of running their lives.

If you do love Writer's Block, and I think we all do sometimes, just as we like being laid up with the virus (under our covers where no one can touch us), remember this: The world feels sorry for you only for three days. After that, no one listens.

Finding the Word Processor That Can Write Short Stories

The age of computers is upon us and clearly they can do remarkable things, an observation not lost on emerging writers, who have come to believe that the computers can, among their remarkable skills, write short stories. And so the question is raised repeatedly in writing seminars: "Shall I buy a word processor?"

It's not a simple question. A word processor can be enormously helpful to a writer—but that is not actually the question being asked. The real question, the underlying question, the subliminal question is this: "Will the machine make me a better writer?" And that question doesn't mean a *more productive writer*. It means in effect: "Will the machine make me more skillful?"

Those who believe that this analogy is ridiculous—that yes, we're all a little crazy in the writing community but not that crazy—might think differently if they listened to the word processor questions in a writing seminar. They evidence an expectation not unlike the lottery player who announces that today's ticket will make him rich. The questions are not practical or constructive as much as they are hopeful. The writers are really hoping that they can rub the side of the word processor and the genie will appear. "Write me three short stories, genie of the computer, one for *The New Yorker*, one for *Esquire* and one for *Partisan Review*."

I would not want to suggest that the professional writer, turning out a novel every year or two or an article every week, should not buy a word processor. Professionals use every kind of writing tool from pencils and yellow pads to 1939 Royal manuals to IBM Selectrics to word processors. They know what works and they use it. But professionals usually do not delude themselves about their writing machinery. Other things perhaps, but not the machines. It's the beginning writers, not fully committed and battling demands on their time, who have come to hope for miracles. Perceiving their problem as related to the writing machine in a manner similar to people who are chronically late always blaming the traffic, they turn to the computer for magic it cannot perform.

"The word processor will allow me to edit as I write," they say. Or, "The word processor will permit me to reproduce manuscripts without retyping." And while these are correct assumptions, they are not exactly what these writers have in mind.

I fear that the word processor is to the writer something like the get-rich-quick scheme is to the investor or the fad diet is to the dieter: a genie in a lamp. The get-rich-quick schemes don't create wealth; the fad diets don't lose weight; and the word processor cannot write short stories. Maybe someday they will, but then a by-line won't be worth having.

Collaborating: For and Against

The most successful collaborations are between people who have a story to tell and don't know how to tell it, and people who *do* know how to tell it but don't have the story.

The most unsuccessful collaborations are between two writers or would-be writers who are not seriously committed to a writing project but think the fun of working together will stimulate the creative energies. What they really want to do is socialize, and a book somewhere in the background gives the socializing a noble purpose.

When two writers think collaboration will supply the sparks, not only does the book not get written but it often ruins the friendship. At the beginning the project is buoyed by anticipation and excitement; much to talk about over white wine at the Friday night cocktail parties. But in time, reality sets in. People ask how the project is progressing and now the discussion becomes embarrassing. If only my collaborator would work harder, we think; if only she supplied the expected inspiration. And on the other side of town the collaborator is saying the same thing.

Successful collaborating is usually an intelligent, businesslike arrangement (or at least it begins that way), often involving a sports or entertainment figure, who has both an interesting story and a name and a photograph that will sell copies. There are hundreds of successful collaborations between writers and celebrities, and indeed there are hundreds of successful collaborations between writers and writers. In each successful arrangement both parties have something special to offer and the union is strengthened by the sum of its parts. None of these arrangements is made because it will be more fun to work together. Fun is not part of a writing commitment.

The collaborations that fail are those that originate out of loneliness or the desire to make a writing project pleasurable. Two writers meet at a workshop or a party and both are thinking about books. They chat and the conversation glows with understanding and camaraderie. "Let's collaborate," one of them says, and the other agrees in an instant. What they are agreeing to, though, is a social arrangement, a way out of the loneliness of writing, a way to have fun. The test of a successful collaboration has not been made. Which special skills does each partner bring? How is the project strengthened by each individual contribution? No—what each partner brings and what each partner wants is the company of the other, and surely there's no argument against pleasant company but it has nothing to do with writing books.

The Deceptions
of the Novel

The most curious and unpredictable adventure in writing is the novel. On one hand it is the ultimate conception, the grand and noble commitment. On the other hand it is dangerous and crippling. Nothing troubles me so much about a writer's future as to hear the beginner announce, "I'm working on my novel."

Even the statement is frightening, "I'm working on *my* novel," as though the important thing is possession rather than creation.

"I'm working on *a* novel" always sounds better. It sounds more like hard work and dedication. It sounds more like reality.

Nevertheless the beginner is magnetized by the novel as Odysseus was lured by the Sirens. The novel has that pull; it is the masterpiece of literature. It is Steinbeck and Jane Austen and Dickens. It is all the things writers think of themselves as, and all the things they aspire to be.

So that first moment when we lift the pen—when we hear those faraway thunder-sounds that call us to the craft—there, right in front of us, beckoning, stands the novel.

It is all finery and elegance. It is all ego that we can't possibly understand. It's the fountain of youth, and Mephistopheles tempting Faust. Yes, it can be evil; it can be destructive. It has buried more writers than it has helped. For every writer who has sat down and written a novel—forget whether it was ever published—there are fifty writers who never finished the job and because of that never wrote anything more than a story here and there.

Yes, there is the lady in Oklahoma City who never tried it before and wrote a best-seller. And there is the policeman in New York who bought a lottery ticket and won a million dollars. It's no argument for playing the lottery and not much of an argument for the novel.

There's nothing wrong with not finishing a novel except that invariably the unfinished work hangs like a lead weight around the writer's neck and prevents him from writing something else.

"I'll come back to my novel," we all say, but somehow we can't.

"I'm working on my novel," we all say, but in truth we aren't.

And if we dare consider the reality of our novels, we find that we have been working on them for five years and they are all half-finished or perhaps two-thirds and nothing much is happening.

There's even glory in that, as there is glory in defeat if the battle has been monumental. At the Saturday night cocktail party it takes us only forty-five seconds to work it into the conversation: "I'm working on my novel." That's status; it really is. That is the badge that we wear and display to the world.

But for every specious moment of glory, there is the price

to pay. The novel is five years old and hasn't been touched in eighteen months. The writer is hoping that the novel will spring out of hiding and somehow get written, but meanwhile he is not writing.

The problem? The enterprise was too monumental. As the Matterhorn is too high to scale and the Sahara is too wide to cross, its very size prevented it from being completed. And when the enterprise collapsed, the writer collapsed with it.

It is very sad because the talent was there—*is* there—and it might have flowered. It might have written a dozen stories or a hundred articles. And *then* it might have written the novel.

Mountain climbers do not, very early on, tackle the Matterhorn, although the Matterhorn always beckons. They are no less climbers for having a healthy respect for the task. Yet writers, once the novel becomes an idea, will attempt any incline. Unlike mountain climbers, they cannot see how much danger is ahead, how much of their future they risk.

I am reminded of the idealist who was constantly working on an invention to replace the gasoline engine or to create the perpetual-motion machine. Every six months it was a different venture: all glorious, all significant, all million-dollar ideas.

And every night he would tell his wife about the inventions, and although his determination was admirable and his goals lofty, the family was continually moving to smaller apartments in poorer neighborhoods.

So that one night, in despair, the wife, who loved her husband dearly and supported him in every venture, said, "Perhaps, John, while you are working on the perpetual-motion machine, and until you do invent it, you might consider taking a part-time job."

It could be argued that if Mrs. Edison had said that, civilization would have been set back a few decades. But only one in millions is Thomas Edison as only one in millions is the lady from Oklahoma City.

Furthermore, and more important, Edison was an inventor before he perfected the incandescent bulb. He didn't spring forth full-blown upon the scene. And if he hadn't invented the bulb, he would still have been an inventor; he would still have worked. And therein lies the key. To have a noble aspiration is fine and important. But to collapse because the effort was Herculean is too great a price to pay.

And the novel *is* Herculean, both in physical and emotional terms. It seems easy. There is so much to write. The first chapter breezes by. The second chapter is effortless as things unfold and characters enter upon the scene. But then development sets in and resolution, and the machinery starts sputtering—then stops—and soon starts rusting. And the writer's ego, wedded to the enterprise, is bruised beyond repair. Better to live in fantasy—"I'm working on my novel"—than to face the cruel reality of a dream never come true.

The romanticists will argue that I ignore the impossible dream. That I place no value on a life spent in search of the ideal. If that were true, then I would be arguing against a life as a writer. To be a writer *at all* is something of an impossible dream. I think, in fact, that I argue *for* the impossible dream but with a plan for attaining it.

No climber attempts the Matterhorn until he has scaled the smaller cliffs. No runner enters the twenty-six-mile Boston Marathon until he has trained over shorter distances. Actually, that is not completely true. Some runners enter the Marathon without ever having run five miles. But they don't complete it. *Entering* is never difficult.

Sound advice never diverted a true lover, and I fear the perils of the novel-form will not dissuade those whose hearts have been pledged. But hearts easily pledged are hearts easily broken. Remember above all that your pledge is not to the novel: not to any single work. The pledge is to be a writer: to fashion words from ideas, to create beauty, to motivate, to inspire. *That* is an aspiration. *That* is a realization of the self, the ultimate flight of the ego, the truth of the creative being.

Multiple Submissions

Writers spend a great deal of time discussing "multiple submissions," and the less we've written the more we discuss it. It is both curious and revealing that beginning writers are more concerned with multiple submissions than with multiple manuscripts. Having written only one or two stories and having emerged from fear of rejection, they are now consumed by how many copies they can make and how many publications they can spread them among.

There are real questions about multiple submissions and real issues involved, but emerging writers are not concerned with them. They are concerned with their identity as writers, and of course that identity is advanced by a published story or article. The identity is not advanced by hard work and a manuscript-a-week writing program because, after all, who knows about it? Everybody knows about a by-line, and if they don't know about it, there is always the Xerox copy that writers mail out the following day to every friend and casual acquaintance.

If anything is clear about beginning and even experienced writers, it is that we want to be writers without having to write. That's forgivable; the identity of "writer" is one of the noblest of professions. The path to get there, however, is one of the rockiest.

So, when the first article is completed, the writer can hardly escape the idea that two submissions, simultaneously, doubles the chance of acceptance, as indeed it does. Of course, a second article also doubles the chance of acceptance, but we all know which sounds easier. It's urgent that the writer understand this because it is so easy to deceive ourselves. Multiple submitting *sounds* like the writer-at-work. (Didn't the instructor say, "Get your manuscripts in the mail"?)

The real issue of multiple or simultaneous submissions is a professional question. It is answered differently by different editors, and it is interpreted differently by different professional writers. It is analyzed in depth by both *The Writer* magazine and *Writer's Digest* about once a year. For the writer of fewer than ten pieces, the question should not be asked unless one of those pieces has an immediate news peg and will get stale. In such event it may be submitted simultaneously, with advice to the publications that this is being done. Otherwise, writers should focus their attention on multiple manuscripts.

The Writer
and the Product

It has been argued that writing seminars should be taught by psychologists. Only psychologists will understand what writers are really talking about when we blame the editors or our collaborators or our word processors for unexplained stretches of nonproduction. But if a psychologist was not available I would choose a businessman: a manufacturer of a product. I do understand how vulgar that sounds: that a person involved in commercial enterprise—in the world of sales promotions and balance sheets—could advise a person involved in creative enterprise. But in fact a businessman quickly learns what writers are painfully slow to recognize: that his emotional system and his *product* can be separated.

A businessman designs a product, shows it to Sears Roebuck, and is turned down flat. So he shows it to J. C. Penney. He sees the turndown as related to the product, not to the person.

A writer creates a product, shows it to Doubleday, and is similarly turned down flat. He sees the rejection as related to the person.

In the first instance the product will be treated in a professional way. It will be presented to the marketplace persistently until it is quite clear that it is unacceptable. And if the product *is* unacceptable it remains a product, and the businessman proceeds to design a new one.

In the second instance the product cannot be detached from the writer's emotional system. It is not only that the product is unacceptable but that the writer is unacceptable.

It should be acknowledged that a short story, woven from the writer's intimate personal experience, is different from a fabric, woven from cotton yarn on the looms of a mill. It should also be acknowledged that if the writer treated his product the same way a manufacturer treats his product, there would never *be* a product. The emotional involvement that grips the writer is the fertile soil from which the product grows. These differences must be understood and respected, but they must not be permitted to immobilize the writer. After the birth pains both products become remarkably similar. They both have to be sold.

The businessman might also instruct the writer in handling affairs in a professional way: money, for instance. A writer is usually intimidated by a discussion of money; a businessman discusses money all the time. Consequently the writer takes what is offered, fair or unfair. He regards negotiating as unnerving and somewhat crass. The businessman, whether he's a corporate president, an editor or a street vendor, is always negotiating; his survival depends on negotiating.

The writer somehow fancies that the marketplace will treat him fairly, but there is a wide latitude for interpreting what is fair. An editor is a businessman; he has a budget and he is employed by a company that must make a profit. Naturally he wants to purchase the services of the writer at the lowest reasonable level. If the writer is unwilling to engage in negotiations, that's what he will get: the lowest reasonable level.

And payment is not the only issue that the writer must confront. There are the *terms* of payment. There is not only the question of how many dollars are to be paid, but *when* they are to be paid, and under what *conditions* they are to be paid.

Certainly a writer should consult an agent or a lawyer for sophisticated negotiations. No one would suggest that an inexperienced writer tangle with an experienced editor on financial matters. But the issue is really this: The writer should not be *afraid* to discuss the business aspects of his product nor should he consider such discussions "commercial." Yes, they *are* commercial, but writers exist in a commercial world.

The businessman can also teach the writer how to deal with *criticism*. Often the writer is so intensely connected to his product that he cannot even evaluate criticism intelligently. What strikes him as flat-out rejection is in fact encouraging. The writer simply cannot absorb the encouraging lines. It is not at all uncommon for a writer to bring a rejection letter to an instructor, and for an instructor to say, "Why, this is not a rejection. They suggest that you cut it to two thousand words and resubmit it." And the writer will say something like "Where does it say that?" or "Yeah, resubmit it, but they don't like the beginning."

The writer's tunnel vision is the same as anyone's tunnel vision when he is deeply involved emotionally. Criticism doesn't sound like criticism, it sounds like character assassination.

It is all because of the product. To the businessman, an inanimate thing involving him seriously, but not threatening his identity. To the writer, an intensely personal matter evoking deep-seated feelings of joy or resentment.

So, writers of America, as unlikely as it sounds, there is something to be learned from the business community. It may not quite understand the subtleties of metaphor and simile, but it knows about the product and it knows about constructive detachment. As unfashionable and pragmatic as that may sound, it is exactly what the writer needs.

The Vacation Theory

Writers collectively share this idea: "I'll write on my vacation," we all say. This acknowledges that we haven't exactly been writing when not on vacation, but after all, who has time? Two weeks of solid vacation time appear on the horizon and we all reasonably assume that with nothing else to do, we'll write. The idea is striking in its simplicity and logic, and it does wonders for our guilt pains during the other fifty weeks.

It is somewhat like this idea: "I'll start a protein diet and I'll lose weight." We start the protein diet but we don't lose weight. Or if we lose some, we gain it right back. In spite of all reason, diets don't seem to work. Neither do vacations.

The answer lies in the writing *pattern*: It is not an effusion

of creative energies, it's a habit. That's a depressing observation and I don't like it any better than you do, but it's
true. Writing is like jogging: when we lay off for three days
we never get back to it.

There is a strict regimen to working and all the successful
professionals acknowledge it. "When do you write?" the
interviewer asks.

"From nine to two, at least five days a week."

It sounds like banking hours and the beginner is aghast.
Did Tolstoy write between nine and two? Did Keats and
Shelley? Did Melville?

Since the idea is distressing, and since we're lazy besides,
we reject it in favor of our vacation theory, which says that
under the swaying palm trees on a secluded curve of white
sand we can hardly help but write. Or at that cabin in the
woods—no telephone, no TV—the angel of inspiration will
appear before us.

It sounds sensible, but it doesn't work. What happens at
the cabin in the woods is that we sit and contemplate the
four walls.

If we're serious about writing, it's important to understand the vacation myth. It's another seduction, another
siren song, leading us astray. The idea of writing may be
glamorous but the craft is mundane. It's hard work; it's
nine to two; it's routine, and there's no escape. Are you
sure you want to be a writer?

Why Do You Want an Agent?

It's eight o'clock in the evening. We are in a "Writing for Publication" seminar, part of the Continuing Education program at a major university. It is the first night, and I have asked for questions, nervously anticipating what the first question might be. And there it is. Seminar after seminar, writers' group after writers' group, the first question is always the same: "Can you tell me how to get an agent?"

The question is troubling. It should be a last question, not a first question, and only very rarely should the writer be asking it.

"Why do you want an agent?" I ask.

"Because I'm working on a novel, and I thought an agent would find me a publisher."

"Is the novel finished or almost finished? Where are you up to?"

"I'm only up to the fourth chapter, but I have it pretty well outlined in my mind."

"Have you had other things published?"

"No, this is my first novel, but I have heard of agents taking and sometimes selling first novels."

"That's true," I answer, "but you aren't there yet. My

guess is that an agent may represent you on a first novel, but only after you establish that you can write one."

It is something of a put-down, and I see a lot of disappointed faces. Another writer says she has five short stories that she would like to give to an agent. Do I think an agent would consider them?

Remember, this is the first night. These are twenty writers who collectively may have had a handful of stories or articles published. There are twenty minds that should be thinking about writing, and they are all thinking about finding agents.

"First you have to write something!" I feel like crying out. But I don't, of course. I explain briefly about agents. Later, when writing dialogue or discovering markets is discussed, these will command only fleeting attention. But AGENTS has each of them ecstatic.

We will not readily admit it, but writers adore the idea of having an agent.

"My agent says that my manuscript needs editing," we announce.

"My agent thinks I should be writing more articles."

"My agent is really enthusiastic about my novel."

It is the ultimate status among writers. To have an agent is to appear professional.

The agent question is worrisome because it means that the writer is off-track. Writers with three chapters of a novel completed should be glued to the novel. Writers with six short stories should be developing their craft, their stamina, their imagination, and their portfolios. *First you become a writer; then you contact an agent.*

Of course we know, from previous smokescreens and delusions, that writers would prefer to become writers without having to write. That way we can prance around in our literary costumes without doing the hard work. That is why writers love to talk about their novels and love even more to talk about their agents.

Here we are at the first session of a ten-week course, and already nobody is thinking about writing. Everybody is thinking about having an agent. What will we think about the second night?

Actually, I'll tell you what we will think about the second night: copyrights, contracts, subsidiary rights, and to how many magazines can one send the same story simultaneously.

Irritated and disappointed, I spend fifteen minutes on agents, promising to return to this toward the end of the course. My posture is negative, although it will soften later on.

"The first thing to consider," I begin, "is not whether you want an agent, but whether an agent wants you." Three students immediately leave for a course in Pottery, across the hall.

"The second thing to consider is certain financial realities. How much money can the agent make? Let's say he sells one of your articles to the *New York Times* Travel Section—quite an accomplishment. The *Times* pays three to four hundred dollars. The agent gets ten percent or thirty-five dollars. That doesn't even keep his water cooler in operation."

You can see how calm and rational I am on this subject.

"There is not one writer in this room who means anything to an agent right now," I holler, and that uses up my fifteen minutes.

During the ninth week we will talk about what an agent *can* do, and I will retreat from my opening cannonfire.

Nobody disputes the importance of agents and the necessity of proper representation.

But initially the writer must be weaned from the agent attraction because it is destructive. It is much more important that the writer understand what agents will *not* do than what they will do.

1. An agent cannot get something published that does not deserve to be published. His knowledge of the marketplace does not mean that he imparts quality to a manuscript. The agent brings the manuscript to the right place at the right time. After that, the manuscript stands on its own.

2. An agent cannot *fix up* a manuscript. It's the job of the writer to deliver a completed, edited manuscript to the agent. Many writers indulge themselves with the idea that even if the manuscript is a visual or a literary mess, the agent will straighten it out. Most likely he will return it.

   An agent will read a manuscript and make constructive suggestions. He will do everything within reason to get the writer to fashion a marketable product. But he must sense the commitment on the part of the writer.

3. An agent is neither psychiatrist nor counselor. The writer who comes to an agent to lean on him emotionally—to call him at home at night, to discuss his crumbling love affairs, to borrow money—is exceeding the boundaries of the relationship. Yes, an agent will be supportive. Yes, he will understand the frustrations of the marketplace. But he is neither friend

nor lover. The writer who seeks that attachment is looking in the wrong place.

4. An agent is in business; he sells his service as doctors and lawyers sell their services. That doesn't mean that the center core of the relationship is entirely how many dollars that agent can earn. Agents represent writers and share the hope that there is more to writing than simply making money.

But the writer cannot expect an agent to ignore the financial realities. An unpublished writer—even a published writer—cannot expect an agent to send around his stories and poetry. Perhaps, after an agent has placed one of the writer's books, the writer might request some help in a difficult market like selling short stories. Many magazines today will not even consider stories that do not come from agents. But as a rule, stories are a financially losing proposition for the agent, and he will represent them only as a favor to the writer or to help develop the writer's reputation.

An agent is a professional representative of quality writing. If that is what the writer is doing, and if he is doing it on a reasonably consistent basis, then he should consult an agent. Agents are easy to find and they will be happy to hear from you if you represent publishable quality now or in the future. You are the very lifeblood of the agent's operation.

Writers can contact the Society of Authors' Representatives, Inc. 39½ Washington Square South, New York, N.Y. 10012. They can look up "Agents" in *Writer's Market* or *Literary Market Place* (LMP). They can ask friends in publishing for suggestions, or they can ask the instructor in their creative writing course. The easy part of a relationship with an agent is finding one.

The hard part is understanding what you really want. If what you really want is to call your best friend and say that you now have an agent, you are headed for trouble.

There is, also, a wrong time and a right time for agents. The wrong time, stated candidly, is before you have become serious about writing. The right time is when you are creating what you believe to be publishable material on a *regular basis*, and simply need a professional to introduce it to the marketplace.

What then is the writer to do who has three chapters completed on a novel? Complete the novel. Three chapters means there is a long way to go.

And what about the writer with six really excellent short stories; how to get them published? Well, the best way is to submit them to quality journals, and to keep submitting them. If they are really excellent, they will eventually reach an editor who will recognize them. The particular advantage of this is that the writer builds credits, and one day, when an agent is approached, the writer can point to all the journals that have accepted the work. That goes a long way toward interesting an agent.

The Redbook Miracle

This actually happened. Judy Cartwright's short story had been rejected by twenty publications. Appropriately discouraged, she asked the writing instructor whether she should finally give up—whether twenty rejections was not proof of her persistence, but at the same time a message that should not be ignored.

"Submit it again," the instructor said.

"But where? There's nowhere left to submit it."

"Where did you submit it first?" the instructor asked.

"To *Redbook*."

"Send it there again."

The writer was astonished. To *Redbook*? *Redbook* had already seen it. She would be embarrassed to submit it again. The other writers in the group agreed, and the unanimous agreement tells so much about the perception of the writer. To the writer the story is a centerpiece in her life. She believes that *Redbook* will remember it.

Consider the reality of the situation: It was sent to *Redbook* twenty "submissions" ago. The cycle of a submission is about five weeks on average, so *Redbook* saw it about a hundred weeks ago—two years ago. In the interim the magazine has received 50,000 manuscripts. Furthermore, even allowing that anyone *could* remember a manuscript from two years ago, is the fiction editor still there? And even allowing that the fiction editor is still there, is the same "reader" still there? (*Redbook*'s stories are first read by readers, not the fiction editor.) And if the same reader is still there, was she the reader who read it two years ago, or was it one of the other five readers? And if she *was* the reader, and if she *is* still there, and if she *can* remember a story she read (or maybe read the first page of) two years ago—so what?

The writer wrapped up the story, sent it on its second journey to *Redbook*, and they bought it for a thousand dollars.

PART II

COMMITMENT

Until one is committed there is hesitancy,
the chance to draw back, always ineffectiveness.
Concerning all acts of initiative (and creation),
there is one elementary truth, the ignorance of which
kills countless ideas and splendid plans:
that the moment one definitely commits oneself,
then Providence moves too.
All sorts of things occur to help one
that would never otherwise have occurred.
A whole stream of events issues from the decision,
raising in one's favor all manner of unforeseen incidents
and meetings and material assistance,
which no man could have dreamt would have come his way.
I have learned a deep respect
for one of Goethe's couplets:

Whatever you can do, or dream you can, begin it.
Boldness has genius, power, and magic in it.

—W. H. Murray

Facing the Commitment

We come now to a turning point in this book where the reader must make a serious decision: Are you going to be published or not? Your immediate reaction is that the matter is out of your reach; of course you would choose to be published if you could.

Well, consider this carefully: You have the choice; the choice is almost entirely in your hands. Am I trying to sell something? Does an ad for a correspondence writing course await you on the following page? No, I have nothing to sell (having already sold you this book), but I do have a premise about which I am certain: Any writer who has read this far—and we have traveled some rocky terrain—can be published. It will require a commitment of time and energy, but the commitment is reasonable; six hours a week will get it done. Surrender one evening of television and your regular bridge or tennis game. Be certain you are *genuinely* willing to give them up; you can't finesse this commitment. It will cost you six real hours. But it will get you into print, that's the trade.

If you make the trade, you have to follow certain disciplines, and the first is that you must write for at least six hours a week. This will result in one manuscript a week: an article, essay, short story, or book chapter. A brilliant article? No, I don't think so, although it *is* possible. Brilliant doesn't matter here. What matters is fifty-two manuscripts a year. You can't do fifty-two manuscripts a year? Of course you can; don't you deliver a manuscript a week in a writing course? Well, never mind; the manuscripts will take care of themselves. Do you want to commit six hours a week or not?

I believe you do, or you wouldn't be reading this book. And if you purchased it accidentally, you wouldn't have gotten this far. Anyone who has fought through the combat zone of the first hundred pages *wants* to be published and is willing to trade the six hours. But how do I know publication will happen?

I know because it has *never not happened.* In writing course after writing course, writers who deliver a manuscript a week for even fifteen weeks always get something published, and almost always within the following three months. I've never known a writer who didn't.

What about a writer who can't write worth a damn? That's possible, but I've rarely found one. Writers know who they are—know they can write—or they don't bother. If you're still reading this epic, you know you can write, and therefore you can be published.

In *The New Yorker?* Wait a minute; nobody promised *The New Yorker.* Nobody promised the top ten markets in America. But the second ten will do very nicely, and I promise a week of marvelous excitement when your piece appears.

So *my* commitment is fairly easy: If a writer with fifteen manuscripts always gets something published, the writer with fifty-two manuscripts has more than three times the chance.

Take the chance. You have come this far because you feel deep down that you are a writer. Don't spend the next five years saying, "I meant to write that story." *Meant to* are the saddest words in the life of an aspiring writer. The time is now; *act* on it. Don't let it pass you by.

> "Whatever you can do, or dream you can, begin it.
> Boldness has genius, power, and magic in it."
>
> —Goethe

The Lure of the Bridge Game

O.K., you have committed six hours a week, perhaps two evenings of three hours each. But it is absolutely certain that on the first evening you will receive a call from your bridge group—actually your former bridge group—and they need a fourth, just for tonight. Yes, they know you have dropped out of the game. Yes, they know you have made this commitment to writing. But couldn't you just help them out this one time?

Now you might be thinking that you will resist this temptation. That having made the commitment and being caught up in the excitement and adventure of serious writing, you will have no difficulty. So I think I should mention that you are in for a surprise. You will think about the bridge game; you will think about the typewriter. You will think about an evening with friends, and you will think about an evening of solitude, loneliness and hard work. And you will feel every nerve in your body urging you to say, "Yes—I'll start the writing commitment tomorrow."

You see, writers don't love to write; we love to have written. We adore the finished manuscript, the critique of a friend, the fantasized phone call from *The New York Times*, the article in print—but we don't want to write it. Writing is nothing but hard work.

We must therefore steel ourselves against the seductions before we start; otherwise we will never resist. Like the smoker who quits forever every night at eleven, only to start again every morning after the first cup of coffee, we will always, if we are not prepared, say yes to the bridge game.

Too bad it must be this way. Too bad we have to compare a writing commitment to a stop-smoking commitment, but best to understand it at the beginning. All right, enough said. The commitment has been made, the temptations will be resisted, the paper rolls into the typewriter and the writer begins.

But of course there is nothing to write about.

Inspiration

Inspiration only knocks. Some writers expect it to break down the door and pull them out of bed.

◆ ◆ ◆

There is nothing to write about—yes—but there is always inspiration. "Inspiration will come to my rescue," thinks the writer, "so I'll just be patient."

How convenient. In one fleeting moment the writer has shifted the burden onto the shoulders of "inspiration," whatever that is—indeed, has even ennobled this self-indulgence by describing it as "patience."

The "nothing to write about" problem will not get solved by inspiration. Not that inspiration doesn't knock, but only that it is an infrequent caller.

This is how inspiration works: You are sitting around quietly and perhaps a bit frustrated when suddenly an idea passes across your mental screen. It is not just an idle thought—it *hits* you, with an electric charge that lights up and energizes your whole body. You can *feel* the energy; you become anxious and nervous, and you are transported to the typewriter by a force almost outside yourself. The voltage is so high—there are so many thoughts—that you fear some will slip away before you can nail them to the page. You write furiously, often brilliantly, with little strain or effort, and with marvelous exuberance. Three or four hours later—although it seems an hour at most—the creative energies abate and you quiet down, but not before the short story has been written. It's a wonderful moment, a visitation, best not thought about while you are there but pure delight to return to in the Betamax of the mind. It happens on occasion, but only on special occasion.

Imagination is not the fuel on which the writer's engine runs because if it were, the car would always be in the garage. We indulge ourselves by assuming that it *is* the fuel—that inspiration runs the creative mechanism. You will often hear "Inspiration" blamed for a long period of nonproduction, usually after the writer has been blaming Writer's Block for a longer period than anyone is willing to believe.

Inspiration is wonderful when it happens, but the writer must develop an approach for the rest of the time. The approach must involve getting something down on the page: something good, mediocre or even bad. It is essential to the writing process that we unlearn all those seductive high school maxims about waiting for inspiration. The wait is simply too long.

But There Is Nothing to Write About —Part I

In the life of a writer there is *always* nothing to write about. "Nothing to write about" is our one-way ticket to the bridge game. Consequently, the first rule of the six-hour writing commitment is that something must be *found* to write about. Anything. The second rule is that you must know what the something *is* before you reach the typewriter. You never sit down at the typewriter and contemplate what you would like to write about. I'll tell you what you would like to write about: nothing.

There is a fairly simple solution: During some of the 162 hours a week that you are not writing, you are obliged to think about and list the subjects you *will* write about. The list must be formal: that is, on paper and pinned to your writing desk.

You might begin with a series of How-to articles; see page 35. It's difficult to convince yourself that you can't write a How-to. You might add to your list a series of Moment-in-Travel essays, those wondrous short adventures or insights that add so much flavor to a trip to Europe, to New Orleans, or to the old neighborhood. They never happen to you? Impossible. They happen on every trip, and they are retold with delight on the first phone call you make on returning.

Then there is the Viewpoint essay: What do you have strong feelings about? Many magazines have Viewpoint pages and every newspaper (remember, a newspaper publishes every day) has either a Viewpoints section or an Op-Ed page. The odds against getting a story in *The Atlantic* may be staggering, but the chances for an article on the various Op-Ed pages of the daily press are quite reasonable.

Your mandatory list should have ten article, story or chapter ideas staring right at you. There are five How-to or Moment-in-Travel articles in every writer's life, but if these two forms don't get you aroused, you might consider what the editors of *Good Housekeeping* are looking for:

"*Most of the articles in every issue are purchased from freelance writers.* We rely upon free lancers as a continuing source of fresh ideas, personal stories, and unique events that we might not otherwise hear about. The major category of articles that we prefer include: *personal-experience pieces* that tell the reader about some inspirational, unique or trend-setting event. . . ."

In a similar vein, *Ladies' Home Journal* suggests articles or essays on "It's not easy to be a woman today" for their "A Woman Today" column.

Woman's Day reports that it is interested in "stories of remarkable women (one who adopted six Downs Syndrome children was featured not long ago) and about medical miracles (a woman who pulled her son out of a coma is a recent example)."

Gentlemen's Quarterly suggests that the best way to break in "is through our columns, especially 'Male Animal' (essays by men on life); 'All About Adam' (nonfiction by women about men); 'Games' (sports); 'Health'; and 'Humor.' "

So in spite of the writer's axiom, "There is nothing to write about," there is *everything* to write about, and the axiom is just one more tired excuse. Being aware, however, is not enough. You need a list and you must choose the subject before sitting down. Then, for three hours, twice a week, you must put words on paper. If the words seem clumsy, never mind. If the words seem foolish, never mind. If the words make no sense—yes, even that—never mind. Words on paper, three hours. Forget everything else.

But There Is Nothing to Write About —Part II

The List—that is, the list of ten or twenty ideas tacked to the writing desk—is more important than the writing. Somehow the writing takes care of itself. The talent is there, and once it starts to express itself in words-on-paper, the story gets completed. But *until* it starts to express itself, ah, that's the problem.

The List, curiously, often appears difficult, usually because the writer tends to contemplate the broad spectrum of possibilities: Love, War and Happiness, and finds the scale too grand to isolate a single, concise idea. The List must therefore be concrete; must sacrifice cosmic dimensions. The How-to article, the Moment-in-Travel article, and the Viewpoint essay tend to narrow the focus. And when you choose the subject before reaching the typewriter, ideally earlier in the day, you bring to the event some inclination and appetite. Sometimes, you actually can't wait to get started.

If the List does not appear and the lure of the bridge game does not disappear, go at once to your nearest stationery store or newsstand and *copy the list right off the magazines on the rack.* Yes, that's it: copy the list. It's not artistic but it works. Focus on the covers of *Cosmopolitan* or *Family Circle* and don't even bother to look inside. There will be three ideas right on the cover; copy the titles word for word. Don't try to improve on them, this is not the moment for imagination. Imagination is back at the typewriter, where unfortunately nothing much is happening because your list is missing. Bring your newly stolen list back to your writing desk and write *those* articles. After all, if *Family Circle* published them they must be pretty good.

Do not buy the magazines or read the articles. You want to copy the titles, not the content.

If "copy the list" seems more crafty than practical, consider a recent issue of *Cosmopolitan.* These are among the titles on the cover:

1. "Twenty-Five Ways to Ignite a Love Affair"

2. "Coping with the Rotten Crisis of Being Forced into a Career Shift"

3. "What to Expect When You're Expecting"

Surely any writer can deliver an article on one of these subjects, maybe all of them. And if the titles simply make you laugh—if your response is "Come *on!*"—then try a parody. "Twenty-Five Ways to Ignite a Love Affair" does seem to invite a whimsical approach, and "Ten Ways" should do very nicely.

The List serves the writer in the same way as the still life or the model serves the artist: it predetermines the subject, thus eliminating one needless roadblock. As the artist arranges a bowl of fruit or flowers, the writer arranges a List: the List is his still life. Indeed, the artist may ultimately distort the model, and so may the writer; the story or article may finally not resemble the original idea at all. But that's where the artist and the writer start, and starting is *critical* to the creative enterprise.

Warming Up

The List of Ideas stares right at you. You've either compiled it or copied it, and no one cares which. You've accepted the realization that you will not be carried on the wings of inspiration. You've chosen your subject, "Ten Ways to Ignite a Love Affair," and you've committed three hours tonight. So here you are, sitting in front of your typewriter, having done everything right, but words are not appearing on paper. What now? Now you must warm up.

Warming up is one of the curiosities of writing; apparently the mechanism doesn't start running on all six cylinders right away. If you don't understand this, you might think something's wrong and you tighten up. Nothing's wrong; you just can't shift into high gear immediately. Why *should* you be able to? Do athletes perform immediately or do they warm up first? Do you function the moment you reach your office, or does it take a half hour and a cup of coffee?

Somehow our systems seem to require warming up before they get into a rhythm, and writing is very much involved with rhythm and momentum. So it's not at all surprising that the typewriter keys are not immediately clicking. It's normal.

As the tennis player rallies before the game begins, so must the writer take a few swings. And as the tennis player is not concerned with where those first balls are going, neither must the writer be concerned with the first paragraph or two. All you're doing is warming up; the rhythm will come.

The first moments are critical: You can sit there, tense and worried, freezing the creative energies, or you can start writing *something*, perhaps something silly. It simply doesn't matter *what* you write; it only matters *that* you write. In five or ten minutes the imagination will heat, the tightness will fade, and a certain spirit and rhythm will take over.

It is something like a locomotive: ponderous, as the wheels first start to turn; fluid and graceful as it gets into motion.

Perhaps this sounds peculiar, but it's easy to find out. Try it. In fact, it works (and therefore who cares what it is). And it works because the writing mechanism is delicate and complicated and terribly misunderstood. Constantly worried about *always being creative*, and constantly awaiting the *angel of inspiration*, it's no wonder that we are emotional wrecks when we confront the typewriter.

"We has met the enemy, and it is us."

Letter to a Friend

Here's a good way to get warmed up: Start a letter to a friend. You have to warm up anyway, so instead of writing something totally aimless (although there's nothing wrong with that), tell your "Ten Ways to Ignite a Love Affair" to your friend Marilyn, who could probably use a little advice on the subject. Who couldn't?

Writers have trouble writing articles or stories, but never letters. We seem to be wonderful letter writers, probably because the pressure of being creative is removed. So choose a friend and start to write, and worry later whether to send it to the friend or to *Cosmopolitan*.

Countless writers have tried this and it works. It always gets the first three paragraphs written and the first three paragraphs are more important than the first three pages.

Write
the Story
Badly

This is to writers what the Hot Line is to alcoholics: crisis intervention. This is to be used only when everything else has failed. Furthermore, it's a trick, a ploy; it doesn't even deserve to be called sound advice. And since we are adults of sound mind and body, we don't need tricks, do we? Well, let's not get into that. Let's simply say that *this trick works* and I am on extremely intimate terms with one writer who uses it all the time.

This is the setting: It is seven o'clock in the evening and we have arrived at our writing desk via a route that has somehow circumvented the kitchen. So we have already saved three hundred calories and are feeling very self-righteous. Not only that, but we have ten story ideas pinned to our writing desk and have already decided (as we must) which of these ideas will tonight be fashioned into an *Atlantic* "first." And not only *that*, but we've been thinking all day about the central character, and can already see him in action and hear him speaking. It sounds more like a *New Yorker* story, we begin to think.

We sit down at the typewriter, position our fingers above the keys, and like a dream sequence in which we scream but no sound emerges, nothing happens: no words appear. Well, for godsakes, we've done everything right; if we can't write a story tonight, we'll never write a story. Enter crisis intervention.

Here's what to do, and remember, this is a *trick*, so don't mention it to your next writing instructor unless he needs a little crisis intervention himself. What to do is: *Write the story badly.* Forget about all that brilliant dialogue your characters were exchanging this afternoon (and which you can't seem to recapture) and just write any old thing. Write it for the pulp magazines; write it for the comic strips. If you think the afternoon soap operas are badly written, write it for them.

But do it. Don't laugh at the idea; start writing. This may be a trick (a device, to be generous) but it works. It has worked for countless writers in countless writing courses (the writers shouldn't have been taking the courses to begin with), and it has produced some wonderful stories. On the other hand, it has produced some dreadful stories, but the ratio of wonderful to dreadful seems to be about the same whether the device was used or not.

Occasionally a writer has returned from such an adventure and remarked at length to the instructor on how clever the idea was and how he laughed all week.

"That's very nice," said the instructor, "but where's the manuscript?"

Don't make *that* mistake. This is an idea, not a comedy routine. It is intended to produce a manuscript.

It works because we all, over a period of time, over the creative hills and valleys, finally hit our stride. We get our share of wonderful and we get our share of dreadful, and it doesn't matter what we set out to do unless we do nothing.

"Looking back, I imagine I was always writing.
Twaddle it was too. But better far write twaddle or
anything, anything, than nothing at all."

—Katherine Mansfield

Continuity

We have agreed to make the commitment and to resist the
bridge game. We have even agreed, perhaps under duress,
that there is something to write about. It leads us to consider how we shall do it, and that leads us to discuss
"continuity."

A writing instructor discussing "continuity" can put a
whole classroom to sleep in fifteen minutes. Continuity has
no charisma. Accordingly, instructors never mention the
subject during the first or second seminar unless the course
is overcrowded. The discussion is certain to send half the
writers to the registrar's office for a refund or more likely
for a transfer to "Meaningful Relationships," which is only
one flight up and includes hugging and kissing and who
knows what else.

Eventually we have to get around to it though, because
continuity is important. It might be defined as the writing
schedule, or the linking together of the working hours of
writing. If "continuity" doesn't empty the classroom, "schedule" is sure to do it. Writers don't write on schedule; they
write when the spirit moves them. If "schedule" somehow
leaves a few brave stragglers, count on "working hours."

There is nothing writers resent so much as hearing their creative efforts described in nine-to-five language. (Curiously, professionals who write every day don't seem to mind.)

So, distasteful as it sounds, continuity must be considered. With six hours a week to work, it matters how the time is divided. It is possible to work six hours in one evening or one hour in each of six evenings. It is possible to work two evenings of three hours each, and it is possible to skip a week and jam the twelve hours into the following week. Only one of these schedules is practical.

If the reader hasn't dozed off, I'd like to explain that writing is involved with both habit and continuity of thought. *Habit* is no different than any other habit: jogging, for example. You get into the routine of running and you stay with it. You break the routine and you don't get back to it so easily.

Continuity of thought is even more important. If you write two or three times a week, you stay connected to your story lines and characters, and they perform on stage in front of you when you are not writing. You are thus involved constantly in your material and can cross the time bridge between Tuesday and Friday without disconnecting. Three days is only an intermission, no different than at a Broadway show. But two weeks breaks down all connections and we start all over, which is not terrible (unless you're writing a book), but neither is it helpful.

So let's see how the six hours might be divided . . . are you still there?

1. *Six hours once a week:* It is very difficult to write steadily for six hours straight; the body's creative energy curve just can't handle it. Yes, there are professionals who manage it, but they are mostly writers

working six hours every day and they have built up their stamina. Writers who attempt it once a week will notice, around the third or fourth hour, that the engine doesn't stay in high gear no matter how inspired they are.

2. *One hour six times a week:* This doesn't work either, primarily because it usually takes part of the hour to get warmed up. Consequently, we would be stopping on a creative up-curve. Pointless.

3. *Twelve hours every other week:* A disconnection. The ideas don't hold together. The inspiration and momentum that we get from staying in touch with our material is lost. No, absolutely no good comes from skipping a week.

4. *Three hours twice a week:* The practical approach, slightly better than two hours three times a week because once we get going, we might as well give it three hours. Our energy sustains, our concentration sustains, and we can generally produce a completed chapter or story. The most productive hours of the three are usually the second and the third.

The failure to develop a continuous working schedule is possibly the writer's largest obstacle. In an eight-week writing course we *have to* deliver manuscripts, so the course dictates the schedule, much in the same way that a final exam dictates a week of constant study and preparation. When the course ends, we all promise ourselves that we will maintain a writing schedule, but something seems to go wrong. Without a deadline, we write a story here and a book chapter there, and somehow time passes and we wonder where it went. A year rolls by, we look with disappointment at our four or five manuscripts, and then the catalogues arrive announcing the new writing courses (which are no different then the old writing courses). We remember how well we wrote during last year's course and we sign up again, saying, "The course will make me write." Probably it will, but what about the other forty-four weeks of the year?

The solution lies in developing, during those other forty-four weeks, a reasonable, attainable, continuous schedule, and the way we arrange that schedule often determines whether we will be eight-week writers or fifty-two-week writers.

The Book Reconsidered

If continuity is important for writers of short pieces—articles, stories and essays—it is essential for writers who attempt a book. Earlier it was argued that a book is a perilous undertaking, but with an understanding of continuity the risk is diminished. I don't want to dissuade a writer from attempting a book; I just don't want the enterprise doomed to failure because the writer plunged in, unaware and unprepared. "Continuity" is preparation.

A book is a continuing experience. What happens in chapter one relates to what happens in chapter seven. When we sit down to write chapter seven, we must hear the voices in chapter one. It is therefore critical that chapters be written within days of each other. We all think we can remember a month later what happened in chapter one. In fact, we might remember the primary action and the biographical sketches, but we lose that subtlety of characterization and event that really distinguishes the work.

Of course we can reread chapters one through six before starting chapter seven, but by the time we finish reading we are in no mood for writing. And furthermore, how do we approach chapter seventeen?

When we are involved with a book, the characters and events must stay with us between Monday and Friday. They develop a life of their own and they live that life in the Monday to Friday soap opera of our minds. Usually, on Friday, we have only to *record* (admittedly with some grace and style) their activity. Writers are always saying, "I can't wait to find out what my characters will do next."

The characters and events will develop their own momentum, but only for three or four days. Then they begin to fade. Not only do they stop acting on our mental stage, but we begin to forget exactly who they are and why they're acting that way. In nonfiction, the result is what one editor calls, with some annoyance, "a string of beads": a series of nicely done but unrelated chapters strung together. Books like that are rejected with the notation, "Would do better as a series of articles."

So yes, if you sense a book inside you, write the book. It is a most wondrous adventure, and finished it is a noble and distinguished achievement. But let it be a book; let it be whole and integrated. Let it connect and let it have the breadth and rhythm, intensity and dare I say grandeur, that a book demands.

Of course it means commitment and discipline—those dreadful words again; of course it demands continuous involvement. But it is a very special kind of experience—a once-in-a-lifetime kind of experience—so let's be ready for it.

> Now he says he wants to be a writer. But when I tell him about the groundwork, the years of going unpublished, the filing cabinet full of false starts and rejected manuscripts, the four years I have been trying to complete just one 135 page novel, his eyes drift and he asks about all the letters and phone calls and the royalties. He is thinking about the time when the preliminaries will be over. But the preliminaries are never over. If it's worth getting there then you never quite make it. He has the facility and the charm, he may even have talent, but he lacks a certain infatuation with toil. He hungers for the goal but not for the struggle.
>
> —Hugh Prather, *Notes on Love and Courage*

PART III

PREPARATION

Tools
of the Trade—
The Typist

A number of weeks have drifted by and your friends have stopped calling you for the bridge game. Indeed, it appears that your friends have stopped calling you altogether. Even your family has taken to wondering aloud what you are doing all by yourself in that room upstairs, and even your measured explanations do not remove that quizzical look, as though this curious behavior, writing, does not quite pass as normal. The day will arrive though—the day of the by-line—when all that will change.

Meanwhile something is happening: In a corner of the room manuscripts are starting to collect, articles and stories that you are quietly excited by. This is the payoff. This is the reward for the commitment, although the best reward—getting published—is still to come.

Many things are needed during these first few months: mailing envelopes, editors' names, magazines and literary journals, but the single thing the writer most often ignores is a typist. A typist is essential; you have six hours a week to spend writing, and there is no sense spending two of those hours retyping manuscripts.

Typists are readily available and not expensive. The best

way to find one is in your own neighborhood. Somewhere within a five-minute walk is someone who will deliver a first-class manuscript and will welcome the income. After an assignment or two, a typist knows exactly what you want—how wide to make the margins, whether to number the pages—and you need only drop the rough draft in the mailbox and receive the finished product, carbon copy included, three days later.

The business or professional office is another possibility. Perhaps there's a typist who would like to earn some extra money typing at home.

If neither the neighborhood nor the office solves the problem, there are typing services. Check any issue of *The Writer* magazine and note the advertisements. For about a dollar fifty per double-spaced page you get a professionally typed manuscript complete with one photocopy. The typing service accepts legibly handwritten or rough-typed copy, corrects minor spelling errors, uses quality bond paper, and returns the manuscript, ready to submit, in two weeks. And since the typist is doing manuscripts regularly, you would hardly need explain the proper format.

I can't overemphasize the importance of a typist. A writer who undertakes the retyping of finished manuscripts sets up a needless obstacle in a world already cluttered with obstacles. There is nothing so discouraging as contemplating a folder of articles-to-submit, and knowing that you have to spend two evenings doing nothing else but typing them.

"How can I submit them when I can't get them typed?" laments the writer. The complaint can only mean two things: Either you don't *want* to submit them because you're afraid to confront the judgment of the marketplace, or you just haven't bothered looking for a typist. Finding a typist is easy. It may cost fifteen dollars a week (a deductible expense if you eventually get paid for the article), and it could mean that you will have to give up the babysitter, but I don't think you will mind after you see your first by-line.

Tools of the Trade— The Basics

Many years ago a book appeared entitled *The Inner Game of Tennis*. It contended that the answer to improving one's tennis game is not by learning how to hold the racquet, but by learning what is going on inside the tennis player. Improving one's writing game is a similar exercise. The basic rules won't lead you onto the printed page; you have to look inside yourself.

So this book does not suggest "How to submit a manuscript." There are a dozen ways and they're all good. Rather it tries to address why we *don't* submit our manuscripts, or why we give up after the first one is rejected.

Still, a few practical approaches are worth passing along, so let me suggest five ideas that are, if not essential, then advisable.

1. *The Elements of Style:* Professor Strunk's and E. B. White's classic little book tells more about writing in fewer pages than any book that has ever been printed.

It is unthinkable that a serious writer should not own *The Elements of Style*.

2. *Writer's Market* or *Literary Market Place:* These are the essential annual reference books, listing all the book publishers, magazines, and literary journals, along with editors' names and editorial requirements. *Writer's Market*, by far the less expensive of the two, costs about $20 and is well worth the investment. They are both available, however, at the library.

3. *The Writer* or *Writer's Digest:* The two monthly magazines specifically written for writers. Either one will do. These magazines publish helpful articles, list current marketplace information, and *appear in your mailbox monthly*. It's the latter event that's so important. The writer can live without articles on writing, and marketplace information is available from *Writer's Market*, but nothing replaces that monthly reminder that we have made a commitment. Somehow it lifts the spirits and points the way to the typewriter. I don't quite know why that happens but I know it does. Just when we're feeling that we can't write another chapter or can't submit another story, the magazine arrives with news of a change in editors at *The Saturday Evening Post*, and somehow we say, "Well, what the hell, I'll send it out one more time."

4. *A Simple Mailing Procedure:* A good stationery or office supply store will sell 10″ by 13″ and 9½″ by 12½″ manila envelopes. The smaller size obviously fits inside the larger size and serves as your self-addressed, stamped envelope (SASE). Include a very brief cov-

ering letter specifying the title of your submission. Protect your manuscript by enclosing it inside a filing folder and be sure the folder fits inside the return envelope. Your manuscript goes out clean and comes back clean, unless it doesn't come back at all, in which case you head for the Champagne.

5. *A Library of Publications:* You soon learn which publications will be interested in your work, and you are therefore interested in those publications. You needn't subscribe but you should have an issue lying around for reference. The popular magazines are available at any newsstand, and the less popular ones you can get by writing for a contributor's copy. Check *Writer's Market.* Some magazines will send a contributor's copy if you send a self-addressed, stamped envelope. If not, enclose three bucks and a mailing sticker; that should do it. With the magazine in hand you can judge its personality, read the columns that run issue after issue, and find out the name of, say, the travel editor from the masthead. You can also determine whether the magazine is what you expected. I know of one writer who had an article accepted by what sounded like a woman's magazine. Perhaps it was, but the women were not exactly attired in the kind of costumes—if indeed they were attired at all—that the name of the magazine suggested. Pity. You get a by-line and you can't send it to anyone.

The Library Slave

It's important to have a library of publications but it's just as important not to become a library slave. We have six hours a week to write, and reading is not writing. Nevertheless, the editorial requirements of the various magazines advise: "The best way to break in is to read the magazine." Editors are justifiably annoyed when they receive an article entitled "The Beaches of St. Tropez" when their readers spend their vacations camping in the Adirondacks. I can document the story of one writer who submitted to an airline magazine an article entitled "The Three-Star Restaurants of France." The editor replied, "We enjoyed your gourmet survey and will add the recommendations to our personal lists, but we *do not fly to France.*"

Editors are correct: read their magazines. But who has time?

It's easy to become a library slave. Here are all these inviting magazines lying around, and who wouldn't rather read an article than write one? And anyway, didn't the editor say we should read the magazine before submitting? Writers are superb at this kind of reasoning, which may go a long way toward explaining why writers are often well read but not always well written. So regardless of all the well-intended advice, *don't* read all those magazines. This will surely endear me to the editors of America, and especially to the one to whom I sent "The Three-Star Restaurants of France."

Don't read the magazines, but do look at them. It requires only five minutes to look at a magazine, and this tunes you in to the editorial "feeling." It doesn't rescue you from submitting an article that they "ran last month," but if you make that mistake, endure the criticism quietly and don't let it dissuade you from submitting to the magazine again. (Editors have short memories, and so would we if we received a thousand manuscripts a month.)

The editorial warnings surround us:

"Writers must read the magazine cover to cover."

"Essential to have a solid familiarity with magazine before submitting."

The warnings cannot be ignored, but blind compliance leads to library slavery—and library slavery leads nowhere.

Word Processors Revisited

In spite of the fact that I am prejudiced against word processors, they are here to stay and we are not. Their major shortcoming—they cannot write short stories—will soon be corrected, and the craft of writing, serving no useful purpose, will join calligraphy and cabinetmaking as something people used to do in the old days. While we're waiting around for one more aspect of our lives to be surrendered to machines, we may as well be friendly and declare a truce.

Even today, in the infancy of the word processor, it's apparent that the contraption can do one or two useful things. Primarily it permits the writer to edit a manuscript without retyping. We have each completed the perfect manuscript, typed and ready to submit—but wait a minute, we want to add two sentences to the first paragraph. With a typewriter the whole manuscript may have to be redone. A word processor solves the problem in a moment. Similarly, it eliminates a paragraph, adds a paragraph, changes a word or a sentence, widens or narrows margins, and adjusts straggler sentences—those annoying last few words of a piece that somehow always seem to topple over onto a last page, all by themselves.

Then, at our command, the machine types a perfect manuscript, which we immediately submit to our favorite editor who returns it in a condition that will be useful only for starting a fire in the outdoor grill. So what! We press the button on the word processor and another perfect manuscript appears. This one is accepted, but the magazine wants 2,500 words reduced to 1,500, and after spending the requisite three hours cursing out the editor and swearing we will never comply, we easily eliminate 1,000 words on the machine.

Next, we use the word processor for query letters. I do advise in a later section to avoid query letters, but I don't say always. Sometimes you have to send the damn things, and a word processor is perfect. We type the query letter and then simply change the editor's name, the publication, and the address, and feed out limitless letters— all the same, of course—to appropriate publications.

For those writers who consider referring to the dictionary as an exercise beneath the artistic temperament, a word processor can be programmed to tap you lightly across the wrist when you misspell.

And for those writers for whom the noise of a typewriter is a serious problem—small apartments, babies who should be asleep—the word processor types quietly. Of course, it doesn't print quietly, but the printing can be done in the morning.

So we have to admit that the device already serves some useful purpose, and as soon as we understand that a processor will not be more creative than an old Royal portable, we can evaluate whether the advantages are worth the $1,500 cost. In the next century, the word processors will decide whether the writers are worth the $1,500 cost.

We Are What We Buy

"Show me the ads and I'll tell you the magazine," claims a writer who has developed a rather special system for studying the marketplace.

I chose a magazine from the rack, leafed through the pages, and announced the advertised products: Aramis

900—Ralph Lauren—The Lean Machine (pumping iron)—Michelob—Camel Lights?

"Esquire," he said.

It could have been a lucky guess, so I asked him another one: Cheer—Virginia Slims—Jell-O—Montgomery Ward—Cover Girl?

"Woman's Day."

"I don't have time to study the magazines," said the writer, "but I must know the marketplace. So I try to tune in to the reader: to her personality, to her economic bracket, to her sense of values. My theory is: *We are what we buy,* and when I understand what the reader buys, she comes into focus. She sort of appears on my mental screen. When I can *see* her, I know what she wants to read, and therefore what the magazine will publish.

"Advertisers and writers have identical interests: to send a message to the reader. The difference is that advertisers have millions to spend on market research while writers can barely afford the price of the magazine. When advertisers choose a magazine, they know exactly who they are selling to. They don't advertise Ralph Lauren in *Woman's Day* if the *Woman's Day* reader buys at Montgomery Ward. So the advertiser does my market research and the reader is identified."

I thought the lesson was over but my friend was just getting warmed up. *"Esquire* and *Woman's Day* present pretty clear audience pictures, but there are subtle distinctions separating all publications. A magazine might advertise the same products as *Woman's Day* and yet have a slight tilt toward the inspirational or the religious: *The Saturday Evening Post,* for example. If you look carefully at its ads you see Jell-O and Cheer, yes, but also Norman Rockwell posters and Centennial plates. The *Woman's Day* reader doesn't exactly fit. If I were doing an article, 'Great Wine Bargains Under Five Dollars,' I might send it to *Woman's Day* but not to *The Saturday Evening Post.* The 'Five Dollars' is right but the 'Wine' is wrong.

"Many magazines might advertise products found in *Esquire* and yet slant off in different directions: *The New Yorker*, for example. To bring the picture of *The New Yorker* reader onto our screen, we would have to observe the subtle differences. The slant would be toward the intellectual. *The New Yorker* might include Aramis 900 but not Camel Lights; more likely Books on Tape. The differences are elusive. Drop a product here and add a product there, and the picture changes. It's like a kaleidoscope: a quarter turn to the right and the image changes; a half turn to the right and it changes dramatically.

"In some cases the same article, essay or story could be submitted to either *Esquire* or *The New Yorker.* In other cases it would be appropriate for only one or the other."

I had the feeling that my friend could go on and on, distinguishing between *House Beautiful* and *House & Garden*, between *Savvy* and *Working Woman*, between *Harper's* and *The Atlantic.* His approach is unique, and while it is not the only way to evaluate a magazine, it does zero in on the essential problem: how to identify the reader.

All too often writers view the women's magazines or the travel magazines as a general blur and consider a manuscript equally suited to *Vogue* and *Woman's Day.* Of course no one *we* know would make such a mistake, but if you think it doesn't happen regularly, ask the editors. A jewelry salesman cannot sell the same line to Bergdorf-Goodman and Woolworth. So, just as you can learn your shopper by looking in the store windows, you can learn your reader by looking at the ads.

"Query First"

We have just completed this terrific article, having crashed through a number of emotional barriers, each bearing a certain resemblance to the Maginot Line. We have evaluated our audience, brought the reader's image into focus, and determined that the article belongs in one of the women's magazines of the Chevrolet rather than the Buick Riviera class. We turn to *Writer's Market* for the editor's name and the magazine's address, and there right in front of us is the warning: "Query first."

So we turn to our second choice, since there are a number of women's magazines in the Chevy class, and there it says: "Submit detailed query first."

We are gripped by a feeling not unlike a tire going flat. We have this article to sell and we know where it belongs, but first we have to query? First we have to ask permission? By the time they answer the query, the subject will be dated.

Besides, what are we to query about? The article is either appropriate or it's not, and the editor will know by the end of the first page. Furthermore, if we have to query to get an invitation, why write the article in the first place? Why not just write the query? This line of reasoning produces a number of spirited query letters but no articles. What then is the truth behind query letters?

The truth is: Try to avoid them, but there is no need to announce who told you so.

Query letters are the battlements behind which beleaguered editors protect themselves, and if *we* were buried by an avalanche of manuscripts every month—some of them not even vaguely related to what the magazine publishes —we would insist upon query letters also. The editors will deny this; they will claim that the query letter helps writers by directing their energies to topics the magazine will consider. The editors are right; they don't want Buick Rivieras if their readers drive Chevys; but meanwhile the writer has completed an article that sounds perfect for any number of magazines. What to do? Write a query letter or submit the article?

There will be some disagreement about this, but if we have the right article for the right market we should take a chance and submit it. Yes, submit it tactfully; acknowledge that a query was recommended. But suggest ever so gently that you had completed the article and just couldn't help feeling it was right for the magazine. You will improve your chances of having it read by sending it to someone lower on the masthead than the executive editor. The fortress around the executive editor's office is difficult to penetrate.

So avoid query letters. There, I've said it. And now will you kindly go out and buy a few copies of this masterwork so I can remain solvent while the editors pin notes on their bulletin boards: No more articles from Leonard S. Bernstein.

PART IV

TO THE MARKETPLACE

"It circulated for five years, through the halls of fifteen publishers, and finally ended up with Vanguard Press, which, as you can see, is rather deep into the alphabet."

—Patrick Dennis, commenting on
his book *Auntie Mame*.

Cutting the
Umbilical Cord

It is the third week of the writing course. Assignments have been completed and evaluated, and many of them are quite good enough to submit for publication. It should be a moment of excitement and anticipation, but no, not exactly—there is an anxiety, a nervous static in the air.

A writer who has written an article that the *Times* Op-Ed page should be delighted to consider raises her hand. "If I send my article to the *Times*," she asks, "how do I know it won't be plagiarized?"

Plagiarized! And we're only into the third week.

"I have a friend," says the writer, "who had an article rejected by a magazine, and in the next issue a very similar article appeared."

Around the room twenty heads are nodding in agreement, not because they have heard similar stories, but because they want very much to believe this. They want to believe that plagiarism is a real threat and that they should therefore keep their manuscripts at home.

"If the magazine ran a similar article in the next issue," observes the instructor, "they couldn't have stolen it from your friend. The next issue was put to bed at least three months before it appeared on the newsstand, months before they even saw your friend's article."

Groans of disappointment from all sides.

The instructor is perplexed; he looks around the room. Who is submitting, he wonders? No one is submitting. He is encountering every known malady from fear of plagiarism to migraine headaches, but what he is really encountering is *cutting the umbilical cord.*

It should come as no surprise. These stories and articles are close to our hearts. They are attached to us in ways that cannot be explained and cannot be understood, not even by the writer. We have given birth to a story: our story, intimate and revealing, and now this very special creation is to be sent into the outside world? No, not likely; at least not yet.

Well, then, where to hide? Perhaps behind *plagiarism.* We can't submit the manuscript, can we, if the idea will be stolen? And yes, ideas have been occasionally stolen, but if we follow that reasoning down the path, it leads to the observation that the manuscript can *never* be submitted.

There are a few more hiding places—there are always a few more hiding places—and the instructor asks another writer whether he has submitted his story to *The Paris Review.* "After I rewrite it," he replies.

And yet another writer claims it is only her first draft, and everyone knows that you don't submit a first draft. "A manuscript can *always* be improved by rewriting, can't it," she asks, not exactly as a question. She is asked to consider her own statement: If a manuscript can always be improved by rewriting, then when can it be submitted? Again the conclusion is never, which is just what the writer wants to hear.

If the writer will not part with her manuscript, pleading plagiarism or rewriting, she is simply unwilling or unable to cut the umbilical cord. She has attached herself to her story with a bond that is probably unhealthy and certainly unprofessional. The problem demands—as it does in the obstetric ward—a radical solution.

We can talk about writers and their roadblocks. We can unravel those self-deluding, self-protective statements like *"But there is nothing to write about."* We can probably even get a manuscript written, although it sometimes requires unconscionable methods. But it all ends right there if the writer will not confront the marketplace. And as we shall soon find out, the marketplace is full of its own indignities (and excitements, let's not forget). If we are writing, we are writing for the marketplace—for publication. Never believe the writers who say they are writing for themselves. We are writing to say something to the world: *The New York Times* has a million readers. We are writing to create a work of art; who would not agree that a short story or a book can be a work of art? We are writing for income, and we are writing so that, below this statement-to-the-world or this work of art, there will be our name. Oh yes, our name; you will never know how beautiful it is until you see it there. So onward to the marketplace, to the combat zone. Tighten your emotional armor, shield yourself against the indignities, and come along.

Introduction
to the
Marketplace

A year ago I received an acceptance from a distinguished literary journal. Their letter read: "What a wonderful story. We're delighted to accept it for publication." I turned to my records to place a large "A" for acceptance next to the submission, and I noticed that the story had been accepted on its forty-third trip to the marketplace. How exciting, and yet how discouraging. A "wonderful" story, and yet forty-two publications didn't think so.

I reviewed the list of the forty-three publications and noted with some pain that this same journal had rejected the story on its fifteenth submission. And then further down the list, I noted that it had rejected it again on its twenty-seventh submission. No, there was no change of editors. My story had simply traveled the rocky road of the world of publications.

Did I get paid for the story? No, I did not get paid; I did not even expect to get paid. I received two free copies of the issue and I knew very well that was all the literary journal could afford.

The world of publications—the marketplace—is tough. It is tough today and it has been tough for centuries. If I told the above story to a group of editors and experienced writers they would yawn, and one of them would say, "I've got a story out on its fifty-third trip."

Hell, *I've* got a story out on its seventy-first trip and it's a damn good story. I only keep count out of some perverse masochism.

The disappointment and humiliation didn't start this year. James Joyce's *Dubliners* was rejected by twenty-two publishers and Irving Stone's *Lust for life* by seventeen. Dr. Seuss suffered twenty-four rejections before being accepted, and e. e. cummings endured twelve rejections on a book of poetry before having it published privately. *A Confederacy of Dunces* by John Kennedy Toole had been rejected so many times that the writer finally gave up. His mother, convinced of the merit of the work, carried on the battle, drumming up support wherever she could find it. It was published at last by the Louisiana State University Press, and in 1980 it won the Pulitzer Prize for fiction. Too late for John Kennedy Toole. Convinced that it would never be published he had killed himself eleven years earlier.

Perhaps the most discouraging story is that of Jerzy Kosinski's novel *Steps*. *Steps* had been published by Random House and had won the National Book Award. Six years later a freelance writer named Chuck Ross, attempting to document the humiliations of the marketplace, typed twenty-one pages of the book, and over a period of time submitted it to fourteen publishers and thirteen agents, all of whom rejected it. One of the fourteen publishers was Random House.

Pain and suffering? Herman Melville was so discouraged by the response to *Moby Dick* and the three novels that followed, that he gave up writing. *Paradise Lost* sold 1,300 copies during its first two years. Emily Dickinson had only seven poems published during her lifetime. Dostoevski wrote,

"I struggle with my debts like Laocoön with the serpent."

The indignities do not end with rejection. Doubleday, reporting on unsolicited manuscripts, says that it receives about 10,000 a year and publishes three or four. The flood of manuscripts at the magazines has been mentioned so many times that to repeat it would be cruel, but every writer knows what it is called: *the slush pile.*

♦ ♦ ♦

Writers who have been published find that their books stay in the bookshops only for weeks. Calvin Trillin, *The New Yorker* writer, advises that his books "have a shelf life somewhere between milk and yogurt." Writers for whom the publisher has arranged a multiple-city tour are always complaining that they get to the city but the books don't.

Even the economics is disheartening. A survey of Authors Guild members indicated that the average income from writing during 1979 was under $5,000. Among the members who are "committed full-time" writers, the average income only rises to $11,000. Consider the writer who has spent two years writing a first novel and is fortunate enough to have it published. The book sells for $15 and 5,000 copies are sold—not an unusual result. The total sales are therefore $75,000 and the writer receives 10 percent or $7,500. If we consider the time involved to write it, the cost of typing and materials, the expense of submitting it, and a possible agent's fee, the writer is probably earning below the minimum wage.

There is the publishers' side of the story and it should be stated. They argue that they don't make money on a first novel either. And as for stocking the bookshops, if the book sold well, the stores would reorder it. If the book doesn't sell, say the publishers, it's not their fault. The writer returns with, "If you spent some money on advertising and promotion, the book would sell." The publishers, who always get the last word, say, "On a five thousand printing we're lucky if we can afford the paper and ink."

So we go round and round and the writers rarely win. There are too many writers, too many books, and only a lukewarm public. It has been that way since Melville, and for all I know it has been that way since Homer. Nobody sees a change around the corner.

This is the marketplace. This is, to put it gently, the world of publishing. This is the arena in which the writer must compete, and these are the rules of combat. Conceding all this disappointment and yes, misery, the excitement of publication is so great that the writers are lining up to play the game.

And, the indignities not withstanding, the game can be played and the game can be won. If that weren't true, then who are all these writers in the magazines, the newspapers, the literary journals and the bookshops? How did *they* get started? They got started by understanding the difficulties and by dealing with them. I don't want to make a case for submitting a short story forty-three times, but suppose I had stopped at forty-two?

I would hardly want to suggest that marketing our manuscripts is anything but difficult, yet it is probably not much more difficult than marketing anything else. Besides, if we have battled our way to the point of finished manuscripts, do we have any choice but to confront the marketplace? It only remains for us to do it wisely and professionally—to see ourselves and our manuscripts clearly—and to follow the path that so many others have successfully traveled.

The Theory
of the
Silver Bullet

A tale out of the Old West offers some insight. It tells of a hero so magnificent, so pure and so inviolate that he could only be brought down by a single silver bullet.

So the outlaws plotted and schemed, and finally fashioned this bullet of pure silver, and waited and waited for their one chance. The chance came, the bullet was fired, and it missed, of course. There was no second chance and the outlaws, having spent months preparing for the moment, crept away, defeated forever.

So THE THEORY OF THE SILVER BULLET means one chance, one glorious chance at success—never to come again. And it is this theory that governs the writer as he approaches the marketplace.

The hero? Why the hero is the editor at Random House or *The New Yorker*, sitting somewhere on a white horse, godlike and untouchable. And the silver bullet? That is the one great manuscript, torn from the heart, shaped and sweated over, until it becomes the very essence of the writer, the very cornerstone of the author's identity.

And the divine silver bullet is fired at the hero, and the writer *knows* that it can't miss because it is his soul that he surrenders. At the very least it will come back with a glowing statement of apology: "A major work of fiction— overstocked momentarily—try again soon."

Instead, it misses, and returns with the inevitable printed card, and it is not a manuscript returned but a whole personal thing. The writer creeps away, defeated forever, and the story goes into the bottom drawer, never again to see the light of day.

I prefer THE BUCKSHOT THEORY.

THE BUCKSHOT THEORY argues that if we fill our rifles with shot and spray that shot all over the place, we have to hit something. It argues that much of being published is having our story on the right desk on the right day. It certainly argues that manuscripts buried in the bottom drawers of America have very little chance at all.

Let's assume that our story is whimsical, and the editor has just emerged from a conference where it was pointed out that the last three issues of the magazine seemed a trifle stiff. She returns to her desk wondering where are the humor writers of yesterday? Doesn't anyone write humor anymore?

Now it happens that there are seventy-four manuscripts piled on her desk but it also happens that this time ours is on top. She turns to the first paragraph—why it's kind of clever. Where has this writer been all these years?

I'll tell you where the writer has been, in the rejection pile. Because if the story was not right on top, or if she had read it after three other whimsical pieces, or if she was rushed or irritated, or if she was thinking they've been running too much humor, the manuscript doesn't seem so clever after all.

THE BUCKSHOT THEORY goes on to state that there are

probably seventy-four editors who might consider our piece and each one has a stack seventy-four manuscripts high. If we get our buckshot into seventy-four piles, one of the shots will be on top.

And of course another shot will not be on top, but it may be on top tomorrow. And another shot may be near the bottom but the editor will love it anyway.

Writers will often say, "*The New Yorker* has just returned my story with a printed rejection slip. What do I do now?" The implication is that they might go on a hunger strike or perhaps look over the edge of a very high cliff.

That is a bit exaggerated. More likely writers will say that the story has been rejected by *The New Yorker, Cosmopolitan, Good Housekeeping, Esquire* and *Harper's*, and what do they do *now?* This suggests that they have suffered more humiliation than they should have a right to expect.

"How about the quarterlies?" the writers are asked. "How about *Partisan Review, Prairie Schooner, Colorado Quarterly?*"

But they are genuinely wounded, and all because the stories are their silver bullets. It will take some doing to convert them to THE BUCKSHOT THEORY.

And THE BUCKSHOT THEORY is so inelegant. Who wants to think of their stories and articles as just so much buckshot? Who wants to think that writing is like selling brushes door-to-door, and the more doors pounded the more brushes sold? After all, this is literature we are involved in; this isn't commerce. Better to think of our stories as silver bullets: messages from the heart and soul.

Well, better to *think* of them as silver bullets perhaps, but better to handle them as buckshot. Buckshot hits. Silver bullets miss.

So if your masterwork is yellowing in the bottom drawer—and if you are yellowing because, after all, how can you write when your greatest story has been rejected by five major markets?—try to think of it this way: How can it get accepted if nobody is looking at it?

The editors of America, however you may imagine them, are not like the Lone Ranger on a white stallion. They are intelligent and competent, but they are neither sacred nor saintly. Like most of us, they spill coffee on their desks, miss deadlines and worry about their jobs.

They are more like a flock of geese, flying all over the literary horizon. One of your shots will hit them. One of them is going to like your story.

But There Are No Markets

Yes, of course, THE BUCKSHOT THEORY, "but there are no markets." Well, O.K., that ends that, so let's go home. In fact, there are *always* markets; it is not possible to exhaust the markets unless the subject becomes dated. (Even if the subject becomes dated, there is always the possibility of turning it into a nostalgia piece.) Writers may not have talent, we may not have endurance, we may not have discipline, but we always have markets.

If we hear ourselves saying, "but there are no markets," the alarm should sound. It is one of those grand illusions, convenient and transparent, and linked to static on the emotional screen. Sometimes allergy season brings it on and sometimes the morbid days of winter when it is hard enough to simply get out of bed. Sometimes it is disappointment: loss of a job, loss of a mate, financial reversal, personal injury. Sometimes it is dreadful insecurity and often it is intense fear of rejection. But one thing it is never, and that is limited markets.

I don't think we want to undergo extended therapy when we hear ourselves saying "no markets," but we do want to recognize that something has gone astray. After all, the lists of publications in *The Writer* are endless. Nevertheless a writer, will read the list of 171 publications using articles and come away complaining that there are no markets.

Earlier I suggested that writing courses could very well be taught by psychologists. They would at least know what they were listening to when they heard "there are no markets." English professors should never teach writing courses. Their reaction to no markets is, "Don't I know it." Of course psychologists may not know a lot about writing dialogue while English professors do, but if I were to choose between dialogue and insight it wouldn't be a difficult choice.

Allow me to point out that there are 44 women's magazines and 127 publications that use poetry listed in *Writer's Market*. The information is right in front of us; it's difficult to miss. You've written a short story? There are merely 110 markets for fiction in *The Writer*, not including literary journals. Sports/Recreation/Conservation and Outdoor markets? I stopped counting at a hundred and I was only up to the letter "P". But you've written a piece on Education? Twenty-two publications listed. Farming and Agriculture? Twenty-nine listings. Book publishers? Into the

hundreds. There is simply nothing we can write—no article, poem, story or book—that faces a limited marketplace.
Even if we were somehow to be rejected by all the publications that might consider, say, a travel article, we would
simply start again at publication number one. It would have
been perhaps two years since our original rejection and
nobody, absolutely nobody, would remember it. (And if
they do remember it, so what?)

One of the best and most often neglected markets is the
newspapers. All newspapers use freelance material, especially on their Opinion and Point-of-View pages. And while
hundred-page magazines publish once a month, hundred-
page newspapers publish every day. *The New York Times*
(to start right at the top) considers freelance material in at
least nine sections: the Op-Ed page, the Sunday regional
Op-Ed pages, the Travel Section, the Financial Section, the
Arts and Leisure Section, the Living Section, the Home
Section, the *Book Review* and the *Magazine*. It is virtually
impossible to write an article or essay that cannot be submitted to *some* section of *The New York Times*.

♦ ♦ ♦

The notion of limitless markets always provokes interesting questions in a writing seminar.

"To how many newspapers can I send the same essay at
the same time, and do I have to tell them what I'm doing?"
asks a writer whose infatuation seems to be with the Xerox
machine rather than with the typewriter.

"Well, how will you feel if your essay appears in two local
newspapers on the same day, word for word?"

"Mortified."

"That's the answer then."

Another writer asks whether you can submit a published article to other publications, letting them know it was previously published. You can of course if you still own the rights to the article, and for a writer publishing on a regular basis it's a good source of additional income. But the instructor is becoming just a bit concerned with the drift of the questions. Now that he has established that there are 171 markets for articles, it appears that the writers intend to send the same article to all 171.

"It might be better for the moment if we concentrated on how many articles we can write and not on how many places we can send each one to. With fifteen or twenty manuscripts completed, it requires a lot of work and organization just to keep them submitted to *different* publications."

The illusion is destroyed. First he convinced them that the markets are endless and now he cautions them about endless markets. "I wonder," he thinks, "whether they'll invite me back to teach this course next year."

Aiming High—Aiming Low

With 171 markets for articles, the marketplace has an enormous range of possibilities. Consequently there are writers who aim too high, and there are writers who aim too low. The former submit only to *The Atlantic* and *The New Yorker* and are stunned by the inevitable rejections. The latter submit only to the local newspapers, often venturing no further than a letter to the editor, and they are elated by an acceptance. An acceptance is always thrilling but there is such a thing as taking the low road to a by-line.

For each writer there is a level of magazine or journal to which we might reasonably aspire, and while there is no harm in taking a shot at *The New Yorker*, there is no point in restricting the article market to ten major publications, certainly not if we stop submitting after the top ten. Similarly, there's no sense in aiming low. To aim low in order to ensure acceptance is to avoid putting one's talent to the test.

A high-road writer commits the sin of arrogance: Nothing below *The New Yorker* seems quite good enough. Her attitude toward the literary journals and the quarterlies is disdainful. The fact that recent issues of *Michigan Quarterly Review* have included poetry by John Updike and fiction by Joyce Carol Oates eludes her. The punishment for the sin of arrogance is reflected in her acceptance record and she is constantly lamenting that it is impossible to have your work accepted anywhere. Her disappointment eventually turns to bitterness: "Do you *like* the stories that *The New Yorker* publishes?", or, "They hire *readers* at *Redbook*, can you imagine?" And her bitterness often turns her away from writing. "What's the use," she says, "only junk gets published anyway."

A low-road writer (there must be a better way to phrase that) commits the sin of excessive humility: "I wouldn't think of submitting to *The New Yorker*," he says. He sends his story to an extremely remote publication (though I want to emphasize that there are few publications that are *too* remote) and it is accepted. The next day he wraps up six more stories and sends them to the same place. The editor accepts all six; he hasn't seen anything this good in years. Surprised by his good fortune, the writer observes that he is not at all excited, and is in fact disappointed and upset. He now thinks that some of those stories might be good enough for *Michigan Quarterly Review* and wishes he could get them back. That is the punishment for the sin of excessive humility.

This same writer, battling an ever-present sense of inadequacy, receives an announcement of a poetry contest. The winners will have their poems published in a distinctive leatherbound anthology. "Enter as many poems as you wish," the invitation reads. He enters three poems and receives a letter that begins: "Congratulations! Your poem is one of the winners in this year's contest and will be included in our forthcoming anthology." The letter goes on to suggest that the other two poems were equally good and are being held for entry in next year's contest. Finally the clincher: The book will be published in six months and advance orders are being taken. It may not be available in bookshops, so don't lose your opportunity to own a copy of this distinguished collection and perhaps to send a few copies to your family and closest friends: price, twenty bucks plus mailing. It does seem like a lot but what the hell, his poem is in it. His poem is included in a poetry anthology.

He begins to fill out the form when he realizes that he must at least inform his family. Result: two copies for his parents plus four copies for their bridge club, or seven copies for $140. The writer is becoming a little nervous: "How come I never heard of this contest before?"

In six months, true to their word, the volumes arrive.

Anxiously the writer opens the package and is delighted to see that yes, this is a real book, leatherbound (or maybe vinyl) with gold letters, and very nicely done. He turns to the Contents page—there is no Contents page. The poems are arranged alphabetically by author. The book has 350 pages and averages three poems to the page, each one straining for breathing space: apparently over a thousand contest winners. Were there any contest losers?

His knees weaken and the writer sits down. The moment of joy turns to a moment of sadness. No, it's not terrible; it's a book after all. But it's not what the writer wanted, not what he expected, and not what he thinks his work deserves. But he sold out, did he not? He let his head be turned by a bit of transparent flattery, and like all of us who are seduced by flattery, he paid the price. Before entering the poetry contest, he might have checked out the anthologist's credentials. Never submit to a publication that you know nothing about.

How does this publication game work? Easily. The anthology publishes 1,000 writers and each writer orders an average of five books for a printing of 5,000 copies. At $20 a book that's $100,000, and the volume is published twice a year. Remember that the publisher receives the full $20 per book. When a standard publisher sells a $20 book (bookshop price), the publisher sells it for $10 and has to pay the writer a 10 percent royalty on the bookshop price, or $2. He therefore nets $8 on a book that is sold for $20. The anthologist nets $20, pays no royalties, accepts no returns, is paid in advance, and prints to order. He doesn't need editors, copy editors, a publicity department or a subsidiary rights department. The anthologist has a profitable business.

◆ ◆ ◆

The writers who aim too high will be frustrated and disillusioned, but they always have a chance to shift gears and
head for a more realistic marketplace. The writers who aim
too low lose that chance. They will have credits but they
will not enjoy them, and deep down they will sense that in
exchange for a few tin medals they have sacrificed a certain
integrity.

Vanity Press

All writers—but especially those who are vulnerable to the
"poetry contest"—eventually hear the siren song of vanity
press, just as the thirsty desert traveler eventually sees a
mirage. We see what we want to see.

Frustrated by rejection and disappointment, we come
upon an advertisement by a publisher who asks to see our
work, who suggests that it might be good enough to be
published. The invitation is irresistible and we don't ask
the obvious question: Why is this publisher *advertising* for
writers? There must be a good reason, we think, and since
our first novel has now been rejected by six houses, why
not give it a try?

If there is a villain in the world of publishing, it is vanity
press, invariably characterized as the Big Bad Wolf in dis-
guise to trick poor Little Red Riding Hood. Yes, the vanity
publishers—let's call them the subsidy publishers—can be

less than forthright. Yes, they can appeal to the frustration and the needs of the writer. Yes, they can make it sound like a standard book publication. But is that any different from the sales pitch of any company? When Brooke Shields crosses the television screen wearing form-fitting jeans by the latest Italian designer, isn't that ad saying, "You can look like this, too."?

And anyway, what is poor Little Red Riding Hood thinking when all this hocus-pocus is going on? What does she suppose is happening when she is asked to underwrite the cost of publication or when she can't find any books by the publisher in the library, or when the publisher is not listed in *Writer's Market* or *Literary Market Place?* If she thinks she is having a book published, don't blame the "publisher."

There's no question that subsidy publishing deals in the theater of illusion, but why are writers so easily deceived? After all, a magician is convincing, but nobody really thinks the lady on stage gets sawn in half. Writers are deceived because they want to be deceived. They want to talk about their books with the same pride and exhilaration as if the publisher were Random House. Not once—not even in a writing seminar (especially not in a writing seminar)—will a writer mention that a book was subsidy-published. It has now been quite firmly established in the writer's mind that the manuscript is part of the library of published books. Never suggest otherwise. The writer will find out soon enough.

That is what's wrong with subsidy publishing: the illusion. It would be so much better if the writer would say, "I had it published by a subsidy house. I tried the marketplace and finally gave up, but it was important to me to have this book in print."

If you understand what you are doing and have reason

to do it, vanity press is a reasonable consideration. The problem is that writers don't quite understand, usually because they don't want to, but partly because the subsidy publisher contributes to the mirage: manuscript submitted, manuscript considered, manuscript accepted—break out the Champagne. In fact, what is happening is that the writer is paying a fee to have a book *printed*.

In the standard publication agreement, the writer receives a royalty based on the retail price, and usually an advance against royalties. There are no reading charges, no design charges, no promotion charges, no charges of any type. In subsidy publishing the writer pays for everything: a book for a price. Sometimes these charges are staged to resemble the standard agreement; for example, the writer might loan the money to the publisher, presumably against future sales. One way or the other, the writer pays up front. Call it what you want.

Again, I have no quarrel with subsidy publishing if writers don't allow themselves to be deceived. But usually they do, and the result is painful. You will be carrying on about your new book at the Saturday night cocktail party when someone will ask the name of the publisher. Having no other choice, you try to bluff it through, assuming that nobody will recognize the name. In fact, someone always does, and that someone, either thoughtlessly or maliciously, says, "Aren't they a vanity press?" The room is quiet, awaiting the response, and the embarrassment is overwhelming.

Further humiliations await the writer: The books are not in the bookshops, there are no reviews, and there is no advertising or promotion. The writer sells the first hundred copies to friends and relatives but the rest of the printing piles up in the basement. The mirage disappears before your eyes.

Perhaps the most painful moment comes when someone says, "Six rejections? William Kennedy's *Ironweed* had thirteen rejections and it won the National Book Award and a Pulitzer Prize." This insensitive observation hits the writer like a brick falling from a forty-story building. "Perhaps it could have been a book," we think. "Perhaps I should have waited." Only a writer who has asked that question can tell you how deep is the pain.

A writer should certainly not turn to subsidy publishing until the standard marketplace is exhausted, and six rejections do not begin to exhaust the possibilities. Surrender after six rejections means the only thing exhausted is the writer.

But let's consider that the writer is not deceived and has really explored the marketplace. There are any number of reasons one might turn to subsidy publishing. The writer:

1. . . . has something important to say and wants a book in which to say it.

2. . . . is an unpublished writer who has written a collection of poetry, probably the single most difficult type of book to get published. (Give it a try, though.)

3. . . . has written a personal memoir or a family history that has no market appeal.

4. . . . has no credentials as an art historian but is nevertheless interested in art history and has written a study of the Italian Renaissance.

5. . . . has a relative—an unpublished writer—very old,

very ill, or possibly deceased, who has written a book. The marketplace, even if it were a possibility, simply doesn't make sense. The endless process of submitting seems inappropriate to the situation.

These are some of the reasons why subsidy publishing might be considered, and there could be a number of others. Far be it for anyone to make final rules about why a book should be a book. It is a deeply personal matter for any writer and there remains only a final word of caution: It is called vanity press because judgment departs and vanity takes over.

Self-Publishing

Writers who turn to vanity press and subsidy publishing should understand that there's another option. It is called *self-publishing* and it means that the writer undertakes the job of producing the book independently. Do-it-yourself publishing, it might be called. It is discussed in detail in *How to Get Happily Published*, by Judith Appelbaum and Nancy Evans, an altogether excellent guide for writers. In short, the writer hires the services necessary to turn a manuscript into a book: editing, typesetting, printing and binding. It can all be done.

The authors mention some very convincing reasons why self-publishing should be considered and include a list of authors who have done it, among them, Edgar Allan Poe, Walt Whitman, Washington Irving and Mark Twain.

An important aspect of self-publishing is this: The writer is never deceived. Unlike subsidy publishing with all its fanfare and sleight-of-hand, the writer comes face to face with the decision. The drums won't roll or the trumpets sound, and no, it's not Harper & Row, but it's O.K. Sometimes it's better than O.K. Sometimes the self-publishing venture starts a book on a trip that leads to thousands of copies sold and *then* it is picked up by a major publisher.

Nevertheless, Harper & Row is preferable, and the writer should not approach self-publishing unless the standard marketplace has been explored. We have agreed that exploration is not defined as five rejections, but if the saturation point *has* been reached and the writer is willing to take on the do-it-yourself job, this is an intelligent, dignified, gratifying way to get your book into print.

Rules of Acceptance—Part I

I assume that everyone has now completed manuscripts when "there is nothing to write about" and has discovered markets when "there are no markets." It follows then that everyone has received or is about to receive an acceptance letter or an acceptance phone call. That's the way it happens. Writers who submit manuscripts on a regular basis get some of those manuscripts accepted—see THE RULE OF TWELVE, page 26.

It is important to remember, in that incredibly exciting moment when the letter or phone call arrives, that we have provided a professional service, a service that has a considerable value. It is therefore not necessary to respond, "Oh my god, I can't believe you're buying my short story!" Of course we're delighted, but we might also want to discuss the terms of the acceptance.

Now I understand that the terms of acceptance are the furthest thing from the writer's mind and that what we would really like to do is thank the editor profusely and ask her which color she would like us to paint her office. But resist; we have rights in this matter. We have written a story that will fill three pages of a magazine that half a million people read. So we needn't apologize for asking some questions and these are some of the questions we should ask:

1. "I'm delighted that you've accepted it. Will I receive payment now or on publication?"

2. "Will it run on the Op-Ed page?" (If we have submitted an article to the Op-Ed page, we should expect it to run there.)

3. "How much will I be paid for the story?" This is always a difficult question but it should be addressed at the time of acceptance. At the time of acceptance, payment can still be discussed. Once the story is in galleys, the publication may pay whatever it chooses. Writers are second-class citizens in the business of publications and our citizenship is so tenuous that we are actually afraid to ask how much we will be paid

for our services. Other professions—carpenters or lawyers, for example—state the price they are charging. Writers not only are afraid to state the price but are afraid to ask.

In fact, if we do ask, and if the answer seems disgracefully inadequate (as it sometimes does), there is nothing wrong with politely saying so. "Please understand, I'm happy to be published, but I have read in *Writer's Market* that you pay between $200 and $500 for short stories." I realize that this seems brazen and that we would expect the editor to hang up the phone, but if the magazine has advertised $200 to $500, she should at least explain the discrepancy. Most likely the editor will respond with something like, "Yes, it does seem a bit low, but your story is only a thousand words," or, "Let me see what I can do. I'll call you back this afternoon." This doesn't necessarily mean that we will get more money for the story, but neither does it mean that the phone will click. The editor wants to buy our manuscript.

Naturally we should use some discretion in our inquiries. A rapid-fire series of questions is inappropriate for a first acceptance to a magazine. The issue of payment requires some tact and judgment; an article that's worth $1,000 at *Playboy* is worth $100 at *The Nation*.

If the writer is concerned that asking questions seems unduly aggressive or even brazen, I would like to suggest that this is the last thing to worry about. Writers are rarely aggressive or brazen. The million-dollar writers may be, and perhaps some agents may be, but writers, if anything, are pushovers. Yes, we may be neurotic, temperamental, disorganized and unreasonable, but not aggressive. So remember to keep your chin up; you're not likely to offend anybody. If you've traveled all the way from article-written to article-submitted to article-accepted, you've got a steel backbone. Protect yourself. Stand up for your manuscript.

Rules of Acceptance—Part II

We have sold an article to a major publication and have been fairly paid. A year goes by and the article does not appear. We call the magazine and are told that there have been changes in the editorial policy and it is no longer certain that the article will be used. We ask that the manuscript be returned but the editor says the publication bought the piece, owns it, and has the right to determine when and if it will be published. The editor offers to return it if the writer will return the payment. Fair or unfair?

An interesting issue, but essentially unfair. The writer is entitled to payment and is entitled to see the article in print. Only one of these rights has been satisfied. It is crucial to the careers of writers that their work appear. The question, "Where have you been recently published?" is asked all the time.

A writer is entitled to fair treatment from a publication, just as a publication is entitled to fair treatment from a writer. Issues arise constantly and each side may have a reasonable position. Since the writer is generally in the weaker position—more dependent on the publication than the publication is on the writer—let's explore some issues and consider what is fair.

◆ ◆ ◆

A publication has accepted an article but the writer has not yet been paid. Again a year goes by and the article does not appear; neither does a check. The writer contacts the magazine and is told that plans have changed and that the article will not be used. The article is returned along with a "kill fee" for one half of the agreed-upon payment. The writer is free to submit the article elsewhere.

A kill fee is a reasonable, if imperfect, solution. The magazine has kept the article for a year, thus limiting its marketability. Surely it owes the writer something, but full payment for an article that the magazine doesn't use and that the writer can still sell would be a bit one-sided.

◆ ◆ ◆

You sell an article or an essay with what you feel is a great title. The editor changes the title without informing you. Fair or unfair?

Fair, although somewhat discourteous. Titles have always remained the province of the editor and they are changed more often than not. A writer who expects a title to be used is most likely to be disappointed. You can insist upon it, but you should understand that you are crossing an editorial boundary line where you are neither qualified nor welcome.

An exception is the short story or the poem. A title is an integral part of the creative character of a work of fiction or poetry and should never be changed without the writer's permission.

♦ ♦ ♦

The publication buys a 2,000-word article and deletes a few internal sentences, perhaps 100 words.

Not unreasonable. There is a certain editorial latitude that the writer must permit.

♦ ♦ ♦

The publication buys a 2,000-word article and has it illustrated. The writer thinks the illustrations are awful and tells the editor that permission should have been granted first.

Unreasonable. Illustrations are a publishing matter. The writer is not really qualified to decide how the article should be presented in the magazine.

♦ ♦ ♦

The writer submits the same book or article to three different publishers at the same time, without informing them. One publisher buys the manuscript. The writer withdraws the manuscript from the other two.

Unfair in my opinion, although there is argument to the contrary. The other two publishers could have spent valuable time considering the manuscript, which finally they cannot purchase. An editor who receives a manuscript submission has the right to assume that it is available. If it is equally available to other editors—first come, first served—all the editors should be informed.

♦ ♦ ♦

Writers need not become paranoid about the editorial practices of publishers. We carry enough emotional baggage as it is. Furthermore, publishers are reasonable—although not always—in their editorial practices, and of all the writer's problems, fair dealing is low on the list. Still, the writer is always in the defensive position, faced by large publishers with considerable editorial and legal resources, who are used to getting what they want. We should try to give the publishers what they want but never at the expense of surrendering something that we feel we must have.

Intimidation by Telephone

This advice alone is worth the price of the book: NEVER MAKE A DECISION ON THE TELEPHONE.

You've submitted this article to a popular women's magazine. Aware of the probabilities, you don't expect an acceptance. So when the editor calls to say they would like to buy it, you're heady with excitement.

"There's one slight problem," says the editor, who has had a while to prepare herself, "we can only use the first half, about five hundred words, and we want to use it as a sidebar [a short vertical column that accompanies another article]. I might be able to get you a by-line, though. That's O.K., isn't it?"

The editor's voice has that slight edge of impatience, suggesting that she doesn't want to discuss this at length;

she simply wants an approval. But you're a bit troubled. You wrote a 1,000-word article and see it as a complete statement, not an amendment to someone else's statement. Furthermore, you want a by-line and the editor is not committing to a by-line. All this races through your mind in seconds, but aware that you are talking to an editor at a major magazine where you have not been previously published, you mumble, "Sure . . . O.K."

Some months later the sidebar runs, the by-line is missing, and you receive a check for $85. You're completely disappointed, even outraged, but there's nothing much to be done about it now. You can call and complain, but since you essentially did agree, complaining at this late date will win you no friends at the magazine.

The solution: NEVER MAKE A DECISION ON THE TELE-PHONE.

No matter what the editor says, no matter what the offer, remember that you're excited, intimidated and unprepared. Simply say, "Can I call you back in an hour?" During the hour, you can consider whether you want to publish half your article as a sidebar and whether you want to insist on a by-line. You can make some notes so you don't forget anything, including a reminder to ask how much they are paying. After all, you're selling something; you have a right to know the price. At a major magazine, even a sidebar is worth $200; maybe settle for $150.

You may want to withdraw the article and, with an hour to calm down and prepare yourself, that is an entirely reasonable request. You submitted a 1,000-word article and you want it published as a 1,000-word article. You have no obligation to cut it, nor should you assume—as writers always do—that if you withdraw it you may never again submit to the publication.

The same is true of a book: NEVER MAKE A DECISION ON THE TELEPHONE. Editors may offer an unacceptable advance. They may suggest a trade paperback edition when you think you want hardcover. They may mention illustrations when you think illustrations are all wrong. They may demand a manuscript completion date that puts you under unnecessary pressure. Of course, ultimately, a written contract governs the terms of a book publication, but nevertheless: Don't agree, even at the beginning, on the telephone. Call back. Tell the editors you're delighted that they're interested, but call them back.

Are there exceptions? There are always exceptions. If you've submitted your first book, a collection of poetry, to Atheneum and an editor calls to accept it, you needn't call back. You would never last the hour anyway.

No Fooling-around Marketing

If the reader is getting battle weary listening to tales of the combat zone and is wondering whether any of these ideas really work, this is important. It is the story of a writer who actually used THE BUCKSHOT THEORY.

Charlie Haddox is an unpublished novelist with credits in such magazines as *Texas Banker*, *Drilling* and *Grit*— hardly the stuff to excite an agent or an editor about a first novel. Reporting in *The Writer*, Haddox writes, "After devoting well over a year to writing my novel, I wasn't about to dilly-dally with the marketing of it!"

Accordingly, Mr. Haddox wrote 139 letters, 40 to publishing houses and 99 to agents. He did not enclose any part of the novel, but briefly described it, mentioned his credits, and asked if they were interested in seeing the manuscript and/or a synopsis. He received 36 positive responses. One of those responses led to an agent, about whom Mr. Haddox writes, "She's convinced she can sell my first novel; so am I."

Here's to you, Charlie Haddox. I hope she sells it and I hope it's a resounding success.

It is possible to look at Mr. Haddox's results optimistically or pessimistically. It is possible to consider that he received 103 rejections from agents and editors who did not entirely know what they were rejecting. But it is possible, indeed essential, to consider that he received 36 positive responses, one of which led to an agent and others to editors who want to see more of the novel. Thirty-six responses! That is quite enough to give the manuscript every chance of being accepted.

I think the critical statement from Mr. Haddox is, "I wasn't about to dilly-dally with the marketing of it!" Yet it is common for writers to spend a year or two of intense effort writing a book and then to give up after submitting it half a dozen times.

Even a dozen times are not nearly enough—even two dozen times. Mr. Haddox received only one positive response out of four proposals. That would translate into six positives on twenty-four attempts: not enough.

So if a writer is thinking, "I sent out two dozen proposals, only an idiot would persist after that," he is not thinking positively or wisely. And not because I say so, with perhaps badgering insistence, but because most editors say so. And every once in a while a Charlie Haddox comes along with documentary evidence.

Musical Chairs

The Charlie Haddox caper, 139 book proposals, addresses the rules of submitting, and if you don't like the rules, you're not obligated to play the game. If you don't mind the rules (because, after all, nobody *likes* them), prepare yourself for a marketing effort that can best be described as playing musical chairs.

The writer is producing a manuscript a week, so after the fifteenth week all fifteen manuscripts have been completed and submitted. (There is no such thing as completing a manuscript and not submitting it.) All fifteen manuscripts are rejected, let's say on the same day. What do we do?

1. Get back into bed.

2. Head for the refrigerator.

3. Give up writing forever.

No, what we do is play musical chairs. We take all fifteen manuscripts and move them one publication to the right, so that they are all out again to the same publications, but each manuscript to a different magazine.

If they all return, we repeat the procedure, moving one turn to the right again and getting all the manuscripts into new chairs: editors' chairs, that is. This is an improvement on musical chairs where one chair is removed after each round. Here, all fifteen manuscripts stay in the game; all fifteen publications stay in the game, and the only thing required is the stamina of a marathon runner.

After the third round we have created forty-five possibilities. If they all return again, we are entitled to one visit to the refrigerator. But it won't happen; some of the manuscripts will be accepted. And by that time we will have written some new manuscripts that will fill the spaces opened by acceptances, because the game of musical chairs goes on and on.

Editors (and how they got that way)

It appears that editors are here to stay, an observation that may not be greeted happily by the community of writers who have decided that editors are single-handedly responsible for all their problems. At any gathering of writers you will hear some hair-raising editor stories. Of course, at any gathering of editors, you will hear some hair-raising writer stories. It is sort of the Hatfields and the McCoys: sometimes all-out war, sometimes a guarded truce.

Before cataloguing the crimes committed by editors—an exercise that could consume a number of pages—let's admit this: If a writer is not publishing, it is not the editor's fault. Writers who have exhausted their Writer's Block alibis soon turn on the editors. "They only publish their friends" is a standard indictment.

Complaining about editors is fair game, but when we start to seriously blame them for our writing problems, we're deluding ourselves. It would be like the unsuccessful actor blaming the directors or the unsuccessful salesman blaming his customers. It's self-deception and self-indulgence and all too convenient. When disenchanted writers are questioned, it turns out that they have written only two pieces during the last year. "What's the sense of writing?" they say. "The editors don't read the stuff anyway."

So before we get to the horror stories, let's concede the major issue: Editors, like doctors, teachers and writers, do their jobs, and not always remarkably well. If writers twist that into an excuse for nonwriting, they make an unfortunate error. Even their writing friends will know the difference between editor horror stories and editors-as-an-excuse. Writers will listen with fascination to the horror stories, but when the discussion turns to, "And that's why I've never been published," you will notice that everyone seems to be going home early.

Here are some documented horror stories:

You submit a manuscript and get no reply. After two months you send a letter of inquiry, naturally with a self-addressed, stamped envelope (SASE); still no reply. After four months you send another letter of inquiry, and after receiving no response to that letter you give up and submit the manuscript to another publication. The new publication accepts it promptly for its October issue and at just about that time the first publication advises that your story is in *its* October issue.

♦ ♦ ♦

Your 2,500-word article is published by a major magazine. Very nice. Their new title is not dreadful, they spell your name correctly, remembering the middle initial, and they send a check. You're reading the article in the magazine and you're quite pleased as you reach the bottom of the second page. You turn the page but the article does not continue. "It must continue somewhere," you think as you frantically flip the pages, but it continues nowhere. The next morning you call the editor, who seems just a bit irritated that you are asking what happened to the rest of your article. "Oh," she says, "we had a space problem."

♦ ♦ ♦

You submit an essay and the editor buys it. They print the essay perfectly in every respect and also list it on the cover. You're delighted until you notice that on the cover they attribute the essay to another writer. A mistake.
"That can never happen," someone says.
Want to bet?

♦ ♦ ♦

You sell what you would like to think is a humorous essay. If it's not humorous it's not anything, and anyway they bought it so they must think so. The essay appears, almost completely rewritten; your entire rhythm, voice and wit changed into the style of the editor.

You call and ask why they didn't return it and allow you to make the changes. "Didn't have time," says the editor, "working against a deadline."

♦ ♦ ♦

You sell a book and the publisher arranges a promotional tour. It is quite difficult for you to manage it—perhaps you have another job—but the publisher says you have to get behind the book. The suggestion is, if you won't, they won't. So you head for Cleveland, the first stop, where you have two radio programs and one television show scheduled. You plug the hell out of the book but there's not a copy to be found in the entire city.

♦ ♦ ♦

If all of this were not quite enough, editors are also famous for holding proposals for six months, manuscripts for nine months, and letters of inquiry forever. They are also responsible for all those printed rejection slips that paper our walls and for not recognizing true genius when they see it.

Finally they are to be blamed for not appreciating what a rewarding experience it must be to work with talented, organized, dependable and well-balanced writers.

Writers
(and how *they* got that way)

It is said that prizefighters, absorbing that relentless battering year after year, finally get punchy. I think that's what happens to writers. When we send those manuscripts out time after time, only to have them returned time after time, it's like going fifteen rounds. No wonder that behind that sensitive and intelligent mask, the brains are rattling around.

How else to explain that:

1. The writer sells a restaurant article to a magazine, inventing an exceedingly clever title like "Remembrance of Things Pasta." The editor calls to tell the writer that she loves the article but has to change the title because it's been done four hundred times in the last two years. The writer screams, "The title is brilliant, and if you don't like it send back the article." The editor refrains from mentioning that the title *was* brilliant two years ago but has ceased to be. She returns to her black coffee, shakes her head, and considers taking a job in the garment center.

2. Writers write "What You Must Know About Your

Mercedes" and send it to *Family Circle*, and then follow with "Improving the Trade-in Value of Your Chevy," which they send to *Town & Country*.

3. Writers call up a busy editor at *Travel & Leisure* and say, "How would you like a piece on Arizona?"

4. Or call their book editor and ask, "When will my review appear in *The New York Times*?" (There are 40,000 books published every year, and the *Times* reviews about 2,500 of them: one in sixteen.)

5. Writers spend the entire first month following a book publication visiting all the bookshops in the state and, when no one is looking, displaying their book at the checkout counter. That's understandable. The interesting part is, we think the bookshop personnel doesn't know what we are doing.

So if people think *editors* are neurotic, let them be introduced to the writers. And if the editors *are* a bit neurotic —and I don't doubt it—this is how they got that way.

Independence

At the beginning of the seminar the instructor wrote these words on the blackboard:

THE PRIMARY OBLIGATION OF THE WRITING INSTRUCTOR IS

_____ _____ _____.

He asked the group to fill in the three missing words and there was no shortage of replies.

"To criticize manuscripts," said one writer.

"Exploring the marketplace," said another.

"Encouraging us to write," said a writer who had snuck in an extra word, but nobody was counting.

"None of the answers is even close," said the instructor as he completed the statement:

THE PRIMARY OBLIGATION OF THE WRITING INSTRUCTOR IS TO ELIMINATE HIMSELF.

Nobody was prepared for the answer because that is not the way a group of writers thinks. A writing seminar is a place for instruction, guidance and support, which the writing instructor is expected to provide.

"I'll try to provide them," he said, "but the single most important thing I have to offer you is independence."

♦ ♦ ♦

The writing community is filled with support systems and all roads lead to dependency. They come in clever disguises: the writing course, the summer conference, the how-to book and the writing instructor. Perhaps the most deceptive is the instructor. He shares an intimate experience with the writer, and that intimacy can cross the boundary line from constructive help to dependency.

One has only to observe the final meeting in a writing course or the last day of a summer workshop to sense the intensity of the bond. One hears constantly repeated, "I don't know how I'll live through next Friday evening."

The involvement is not difficult to understand. The instructor is seen, not surprisingly, as a mentor, and he is credited with absolute critical judgment. Furthermore, he relates to writers in the most personal way: to their manuscripts and all the anxiety that surrounds them, and through their manuscripts to the backroads and corners of their private lives.

The instructor is drawn into this web. Flattered by all the attention and adulation, he perceives himself as sitting on the high altar and understandably finds it quite comfortable. Well, why not? All these writers hanging on to everything he says, when in fact his last book has sold 1,200 copies and he can't even get his editor on the phone. It is at this moment, motivated by an exaggerated sense of self-importance, that he makes a critical error. He announces that he is repeating the course in the spring, and all twenty-five writers sign up on the spot.

So the instructor, dependent on the writers, indulges his ego. And the writers, frantic that they will not survive without their mentor, sign up to learn the same things all over again. It is all wrong.

Finally a writer has to become a writer, not a camp follower of writing courses. Never mind that the atmosphere crackles with all that intellectual electricity. Never mind that it *seems* like writing is going on. The activity in writing-for-publication can be easily measured: how much writing and how much submitting?

Yes, take the writing course; there are excellent writing courses. But when the course is over and you find yourself hoping that the instructor will repeat it in the spring, watch out. The magnetic forces that pull instructor to writer and writer to instructor must be resisted. *The primary obligation of the writing instructor is to eliminate himself.*

♦ ♦ ♦

In another seminar the instructor will write on the blackboard:

THE MOST IMPORTANT WEEK IN A
TEN-WEEK WRITING COURSE IS

——————————— ———————————.

The writers will respond with "the first" or "the tenth" —reasonable answers to an unreasonable question—but they are not getting this one right either. The important week in a ten-week writing course is the eleventh. Of course it is.

So if you are dazzled by the summer conferences with

their cast of well-known writers and editors, consider this: When writers start writing, they stop attending conferences. Finally, only one thing works for the writer: writing. All the trappings—the seminars, the collaborating, the how-to books, the passing around of manuscripts—are just so much costume and parade. A book chapter, a short story, a solid paragraph even, blows all that intellectual pomp away in the wind. However painful, writing is what matters, and it matters so much that there are few satisfactions that compare to it, few thrills that match a completed story.

I know a writer exceedingly well who spent a night happily in Penn Station, napping cautiously among the derelicts, waiting . . . waiting for the 3:00 a.m. edition of *The New York Times* to see his first article on the Op-Ed page. And a hundred articles later I'm not sure we wouldn't find him there again. You see, the excitement never ends.

About the Author

LEONARD S. BERNSTEIN, between the hours of nine and five, is a manufacturer of children's apparel and between five and nine, a writer. His published works include a volume of poetry, a book about the garment industry, a travel book, *The Official Guide to Wine Snobbery* (Morrow, 1982), and articles and short stories in many periodicals. He has taught writing courses at the State University of New York at Stony Brook and Hofstra University for ten years. He is a graduate of the University of Michigan and lives with his wife in Westbury, New York.